LIFE DOES NOT COME WITH GUARANTEES

LIFE DOES NOT COME WITH GUARANTEES

◆

*A Story
of Love,
Loneliness,
Abuse,
and Faith*

Germaine L. Allen

iUniverse, Inc.
New York Lincoln Shanghai

LIFE DOES NOT COME WITH GUARANTEES
A Story of Love, Loneliness, Abuse, and Faith

Copyright © 2006 by Germaine L. Allen

All rights reserved. No part of this book may be used or reproduced by any means, graphic, electronic, or mechanical, including photocopying, recording, taping or by any information storage retrieval system without the written permission of the publisher except in the case of brief quotations embodied in critical articles and reviews.

iUniverse books may be ordered through booksellers or by contacting:

iUniverse
2021 Pine Lake Road, Suite 100
Lincoln, NE 68512
www.iuniverse.com
1-800-Authors (1-800-288-4677)

ISBN-13: 978-0-595-38691-8 (pbk)
ISBN-13: 978-0-595-83074-9 (ebk)
ISBN-10: 0-595-38691-1 (pbk)
ISBN-10: 0-595-83074-9 (ebk)

Printed in the United States of America

Contents

Preface vii

Chapter 1	The Early Years 1
Chapter 2	Newly Married 7
Chapter 3	And Baby Makes Three 19
Chapter 4	It's a Boy 25
Chapter 5	Back to California 29
Chapter 6	Heart Trouble 35
Chapter 7	Military Funeral 41
Chapter 8	Farewell to a Friend 49
Chapter 9	A Big Move and Even Bigger Surprise 59
Chapter 10	Abuse 71
Chapter 11	Abuse and Meanness 77
Chapter 12	Practical Joker 83
Chapter 13	The Wedding 93
Chapter 14	The Move to Wisconsin 103
Chapter 15	Payback for Practical Jokes 111
Chapter 16	Ultimate Betrayal 123
Chapter 17	Renewing My Faith 133
Chapter 18	A Real Test of Faith 141

CHAPTER 19	My Best Friend Returns	149
CHAPTER 20	Another Betrayal	153
CHAPTER 21	The Final Straw	161
CHAPTER 22	Good Samaritan	167
CHAPTER 23	Soul Mate	173
CHAPTER 24	Apology	183

Preface

People never know where their lives will take them. When I was growing up, I thought I would have a very normal adult life. I thought I would graduate from high school, get married, raise a family, and go through life like I imagined life should be. But God had different plans for me. He led me through many experiences so that I could put them on paper. I truly feel that to write this book is my purpose on this earth.

My story is one of love, loneliness, abuse, and faith. I loved many times but was lonely a good percentage of the time. All five of my children were born without their dad by my side. I was emotionally abused for years but never gave up faith that some day I would find peace and happiness.

I am not a professional author. For thirty years I tried to write this book but had to stop many times. It was too painful reliving it all. It was God's hand that helped me get it done. I was even led to the place where I knew it was the ending. It was the ending God wanted. I feel if I can help just one person get back on the right path, I will have accomplished what was asked of me.

In writing my story, it is not, nor has it ever been, my intention to hurt the people who were in my life. These are simply the memoirs of my life as I saw it and lived it.

I dedicate this book to my mother, Emma Luckow, whose strength and wisdom gave me the courage and determination to carry on at each turning point in my life. She was always foremost in my mind when tragedy struck. I was constantly asking myself, "What would mother have done to get through this? What would she want me to do?" I have great admiration and respect for her. I hope the day comes when my children can say the same for me.

I also dedicate this book to my children who gave me the reasons to go on and see beyond life's struggles and disappointments. They are the ones that made me who I am today and gave me the courage to write this story. I have always felt that my children have the potential to be strong during any life crisis but could also completely fall apart at the first sign of crisis. As all mothers do, of course I hope that they will all be strong and handle anything life hands them. It takes inner strength, faith, and determination to get through some of life's struggles. I can only pray they have learned that from me through the years.

Diana Lynn, my oldest daughter, was with me through most of my life experiences and has been my tower of strength. She always felt like she must be a second mother, a super mom even—strong and wise. And yet, she seemed so vulnerable and unsure about her own life as an adult. Her life began to parallel mine. You may someday read her version of what our lives were like during those turbulent years and then about her life as an adult.

Leary Arthur, my oldest son, always seemed to be able to smile and maintain a sense of humor through whatever was happening to us. Sometimes I wondered if he didn't go into his own world and block out what was happening so it wouldn't be so painful. Although he has a family of his own now, I wonder if that other world is still there waiting for him when he needs to go there.

Michael Larry, my second son, seemed to have a zest for life and all the things it could bring him. He loves his freedom and independence. Michael got a second chance at life and views it differently than the others.

Cindy Lou, my second daughter, is a good mother to her five children. As a teenager, Cindy felt rebellious and at times I was her enemy. I believe that as she developed into an adult she realized I wasn't the enemy after all and regrets the time wasted not having the mother-daughter relationship that we have now and that she has with her own daughters.

Laura Lee, my youngest daughter, breezed through most of our turmoil without a care. She was the shining star of the family, with a smile to match, and was oblivious to most of the turmoil. Much of it predated her, and the rest she was too young to remember.

Todd and Terry Lisowe, although not my biological sons, will always be my sons as well. They will always be a part of my family and have a special place in my heart. I don't know whether or not they totally understand why life was the way it was, especially the way it was when they were children.

I also need to mention a very special friend, Tom McCue, whom I had known since grade school. Without his help, his shoulder, and his kindness, I might have ended up in a mental institution. Tom had such a big heart and was kind to everyone. He was the one who said to me, during one of my life crises, "Life does not come with guarantees for happiness; take it whenever you find it." He encouraged me to write this book in order to find peace with it all. Tom was always there for me no matter what. I sincerely thank him from the bottom of my heart. The Good Lord called him home on April 27, 2001, and I know he has found peace.

Some people go through life with very few tragedies. Others seem to get what they may deem as more than their share. God put us on this earth with a purpose. As I said earlier, I have always felt my purpose was to write this book.

I prayed for guidance to write what I needed to write, to get the story told correctly. I was not always proud of things I had done, and I am certain my children will have many questions when they read the story. But my life was what it was, and the story needs to be told. I hope they will understand that I truly loved them all and did what I had to do, in some cases, just to survive.

Perhaps the story will help my children forgive those that have hurt them and the abuse they endured. Forgiving does not condone what was done, but it merely gives closure in their hearts to move on in life without the burden of hatred and anger. I can't make the memory go away, but just hope that it will heal someday.

As you read my story you may wonder how someone with any brains could have tolerated what I put up with. My only answer is that when you are in love, you allow yourself to do things you would never do otherwise. That doesn't mean you accept what is going on, it merely means you tolerate it to keep your love intact. Certainly, it's not always the wisest of decisions.

1
The Early Years

My childhood was good. My mom and dad, Emma, and Arno were hardworking parents who loved and cared for their family. We weren't rich, but also weren't poor. The 1940s and 1950s were a good time to grow up. We didn't worry about school shootings like people do now. And we didn't have to worry that much about drugs, although I am sure they were out there. Life was good. I had one older sister, Geraldine, and one younger brother, Arthur, so I considered us the average family.

As a child, I was sick a good percentage of the time. My tonsils were the main problem and, therefore, I caught all the viruses that were out there. I was so thin the wind could blow me away. In the 1940s doctors waited until a child was at least five years old before they removed tonsils; however, they decided to remove my tonsils when I was only four, because I was always sick and could not eat properly, and it was costing the family so much to have the doctor come over all the time. Yes, in those days the doctor would make house calls. He would come right to the house with his little black doctor bag.

I must admit, however, that I took full advantage of being ill all the time. If I didn't want to go to school, I would fake being sick. I knew that my grandmother, who lived just a few houses north of us, would come over and lavish attention on me. She brought new coloring books, ice cream, cookies, soda, or whatever I wanted. I was such a selfish child that I never realized that my grandmother did not do this for my brother or sister—just me.

My sister was close to my mom, and my brother was close to my dad, so I felt like I wasn't close to anybody. Being the middle child, I thought I was not as loved as my brother and sister. Children can be so blind. In reality, I was so spoiled by my grandmother that my mom and dad had to pay special attention to my brother and sister in an attempt to make up for the hurt my brother and sister felt about my grandmother lavishing me with all the good stuff. I apologize to both of them. I am sorry they had to endure this treatment because of my selfishness.

One time when I faked being ill and my grandmother came over to watch me while Mom went to work, Mom must have suspected I was faking. When she got home from work, she called the doctor to come to the house. Mom told me if I wasn't really sick, I was going to get a good spanking. Talk about scared! I was so worried because I knew I wasn't sick. I guess fear took over because I actually did have a slight fever when the doctor checked me. I didn't pull that stunt again.

Another event I remember from my childhood took place when I was seven or eight years old. I was walking home from school with some friends when we heard sirens from a fire truck. As we got to my corner, I said flippantly, "I hope it's my house that's on fire." To my astonishment the fire was at my house, but luckily it was only in the garage. I was so ashamed that I had said something that stupid. I remember praying that night and telling God that I was sorry for wishing for such a bad thing. I promised God I would be very careful about what I wished for from then on. I never told my mom and dad that I had hoped the fire was at our house. I knew they would have been disappointed in me.

The lessons I learned from my childhood were to be honest and to think before I speak.

My preteen years were full of showing off and trying to get attention from my friends. Also, boys didn't seem so dumb anymore and actually started to look special. My very first deep love began when I was about eleven years old. His name was Tom Hed. He was not a good student, but my heart was not looking for a scholar. It was looking for someone who loved life, was fun to be around, and was the best looking boy in the whole school. I never thought love could really be that strong so young, but I remember it very well. I would make a game out of knowing when and what time he was walking to school. I, of course, would just happen to be there walking, too. My locker was next to his, as in those days, lockers, and usually desks, were assigned alphabetically. So in most classes, we were either next to each other or within one or two students of each other. I would dream about Tom and plan my day around where I thought he would be next.

When I was twelve years old, my grandmother gave me a diary for a birthday present. I never wrote my innermost secrets in it because I was afraid someone would find it, read it, and perhaps laugh at me. But, I carried it with me everywhere. One day I left my diary in my locker, and when I went to get it after school, it was gone. Thinking I might have dropped it someplace, I asked several friends if they'd seen it. No one knew where it was. The very next day, the diary was back in my locker with a message written in it. The message, written in pencil, stated that I should admit that I was in love with Tom Hed. I erased the message and was flustered and embarrassed that someone knew my innermost feelings. For about a week after that I left the book at home, but then I returned it to my locker. Again the diary disappeared and was returned the next day with the same message, only in ink this time. I accused my best friend Darla Williams of taking my diary, but she denied even knowing my locker combination. Since someone was obviously looking in my book, I decided to write back. I told them they were wrong and asked them to please stop writing in my book and to leave it alone. The next day my words were crossed off and the same message appeared. I tore the page out because I was embarrassed. I didn't have a clue about who was doing this, and I wanted my secret love to stay secret. The very next day, a new page was started with the same message, so from then on I left the diary at home. I was embarrassed to even discuss it further with anyone.

My secret relationship stayed secret, or so I thought, over several years. I had such deep feelings for Tom that even as young as I was, as an adult today, I truly believe I was in love, then as a child. I continued to be where I thought he might be—ice-skating at the local park in the winter, swimming at the beach in the summer. Wherever I thought he might be, I made every effort to be there.

In the summer when I was fifteen years old, Tom stopped at my house with his motorcycle. I was sitting on the front porch and was shocked to see him there. He asked me to go for a ride. My heart was racing, and I wanted to go so badly, but I told him I had to ask my mom first. My mom said she had work for me to do, but maybe some other day. I sadly told Tom I couldn't go that day but would love to go with him another time. He said OK and drove off.

I was ecstatic that he even stopped at my house. *Could it be he cares about me, too?* I wondered. I was in love and floating on a cloud with stars in my eyes because just maybe after all these years my dream was coming true. *Maybe he's the one writing in the book from my locker and wants me to admit I care about him*, I thought. Then he would have known. After all, his locker was next to mine; maybe he knew the combination. I was guessing, but I was sure hoping this was the case. I knew he could have a lot of girl friends because he was so cute, and here he was asking me. Wow! I hoped we could be together soon even if it was just for a ride.

That same evening we heard on the news that Tom had been in an accident and had died. He had been riding his motorcycle on the highway when he hit some gravel and was thrown off onto the road. He had broken his neck. I was devastated and crushed. My first true love who I had finally made a connection with was now gone, and we would never get to take that ride together. I realized then that life would never be the same for me again. I might have died also, had I gone on that ride with him. Apparently, the accident took place shortly after he had left my house. It was not my destiny to go on that ride. I felt empty inside and wished I had died with him. I was going to miss him so much. *How could this happen?* He was too young to die. I was numb for days and couldn't talk to anyone about it. Who would believe a fifteen-year-old was in love—or was I? Is that what love is supposed to be—wanting to be near a person every minute of every day; wanting to know what they think and how they feel; dreaming about them; visualizing life as their soul mate? I guess some might have called it puppy love because of my age, but that's not how I perceived it. My feelings were real and my devastation was real, too.

I felt alone and unable to talk to anyone about this tragedy in my life. My sister, Geraldine, seemed to be in her own world. She was so beautiful. Her skin was peachy clean and perfect unlike other teenagers. She also had perfect teeth; mine were large and uneven. She was tall and thin. I always envied her because I thought she was pretty enough to be a model. But we weren't alike or even close enough to discuss our feelings and dreams.

My brother, Arthur, well, he was my younger brother. What would he know? I certainly wasn't going to confide in him. Besides, he was a boy and, I figured, wouldn't understand.

I learned at an early age that life could be very harsh. One minute you are happy and in love, the next you are empty and alone. For years after that, I dreamt about Tom at least two or three times a week. Even now he is still occasionally in my dreams.

The next few years seemed like a blur. My sister got married; I went to high school, had a part-time job, and just kept on living an average life. As a teenager I was not popular. I dated a boy for a short time, but it was not meant to be.

Tom McCue was a trusted friend and whenever I needed help with something, I asked him. He was only two months older than I was, but he seemed so much wiser. He was so kind and always seemed to know the answer to whatever was troubling me. I didn't think of him as a boyfriend, just a very special friend.

One summer, I was getting headstrong and, like every teenager, felt my parents didn't understand me. My best friend Marlene Pirrung came over and wanted me to leave with her. She wanted to go see her boyfriend. My mom said that I had to stay home. I became rebellious and left with Marlene anyway. After I left the house, I was afraid. I had left without permission and, in my mind; it meant that I had run away. I went to my sister's house and explained what I had done. She said I should go home immediately, and she would not go against Mom and Dad by letting me stay with her. I walked from there to my friend Pat Molitor's house. It was getting dark outside, and I was more afraid than ever. *Where can I go? Where can I stay? What will I do?* Pat's mom said I could not stay there either and tried to convince me to call home because she was certain my parents were very worried about me.

The only person left to call that I was certain would help me was Tom McCue. I called him and told him I had run away from home and needed a place to stay. He asked me where I was and told me to stay there, that he would pick me up when he came into town to get his mom from work. I was relieved to know someone was going to help me. Instead, Tom called my parents and told them where I was. My dad came and got me. Dad was very angry with me for making them worry like that and disobeying my mom. I told my dad I thought they wouldn't care. His response to that comment was, "You are correct, you just didn't think."

I was confined to the house all summer as my punishment. My vacation consisted of a two-week visit to my other grandmother's farm up north. Instead of having fun with my friends, I was stuck on the farm with nothing to do. My summer was ruined.

I was angry with Tom for several years for doing that to me. I was angry with him for something I had done to myself. But he did the right thing by calling my parents and he knew I would eventually realize that. He was a true friend. It was a blessing in disguise for my own safety. As time went by, Tom and I and all our friends drifted apart and went our separate ways.

2
Newly Married

In 1958 I was seventeen, and in my junior year of high school. That spring a friend of mine introduced me to Larry Dean Allen. Larry was nineteen, in the United States Navy, and stationed aboard the USS *Ely*, the ship that docked at the United States Coast Guard station on South Eighth Street in Sheboygan.

Larry was interesting, cute, and fun. He was from Yuma, Colorado, and since I had never been out of Wisconsin I was fascinated by his country drawl and the stories of his travels. He was not like the boys in school.

That same year we became a couple. Around Christmastime, Larry asked me if I would like to meet his parents. He was going home to Colorado for a visit and wanted me to go, too. The plan was for us to travel to Yuma, Colorado, by train for spring break during my senior year. Since I would be eighteen on October 4, 1958, my parents let me decide if I wanted to go. I had their blessing. They really liked Larry and hoped our relationship would turn into marriage.

On Valentine's Day in 1959, Larry asked me to marry him and gave me an engagement ring. We would be going to Colorado to see his parents soon, and he thought it would be a nice surprise for them as well. Of course I would finish school first, and we would marry in June after I graduated.

I was very excited to finally leave Wisconsin, and the trip to Colorado was fun. It was the first train ride I had ever gone on, and I trusted Larry to keep us safe. Larry's parents, Leary and Helen, were very pleasant and welcomed me with open arms. I thought Larry's one sister, Elaine, was very attractive and smart.

Yuma was a very small town, with a nice, country neighborhood atmosphere, and everyone was very friendly. Larry took me to Yuma High, the high school he had attended. I was very surprised to see pictures of him all over the school walls. He was the only four-year letterman in his school, and he had been very popular. He had been homecoming king several years in a row, and his homecoming queen was his high school girlfriend, Deanna.

Larry found his high school sweater at home. He asked if I wanted to wear it. I was ecstatic. The sweater was red and had all sorts of emblems on it from four years of wrestling and football. I was pleased and thought, *It will be great to wear this to my high school. Everyone will be asking me about it and it will attract a lot of attention.* I was floating on air. Not only was I going to be graduating from high school soon, but also I was engaged to be married and was looking forward to being a navy wife and traveling to wherever Larry's job took us. Life seemed good.

On the train on the way back to Wisconsin, Larry explained to me why he was in the navy. Apparently he not only was popular in school, but also mischievous and rebellious. According to Larry, when he and some friends had gone to a movie, he got bored, skipped out of the movie, stripped a car, and then went back to the movie. Somehow the law caught up with him, and he ended up in court. The judge told Larry he had two choices. He could either go to jail or join the military. Larry said he didn't want to sit in jail, so he joined the navy. He told me he was glad the judge had given him a break because he felt boot camp gave him some direction and meaning in life. And, it got him out of Yuma to start a new life of his own as an adult.

Larry and I saw each other as often as we could. With his going out to sea and my going to school and working part-time, our time together was limited. We continued to make plans for our wedding. It would be a small wedding with my sister, Geraldine, and her husband, Ed, as our attendants. The reception would be held at Mom and Dad's house with a small gathering of relatives. Larry's parents were coming, too, but would be the only relatives in attendance from his side of the family.

The closer I got to getting married the more frightened I became. I was eighteen years old, not totally out of school yet, and engaged to a man that I hardly knew. Something was not right. Was I truly in love or was I visualizing the excitement of getting married and traveling? I had to be sure. This was a decision that I would have to live with for the rest of my life. It was my first big choice as an adult, yet I still felt like a little girl.

In early April of 1959, I finally decided I had better speak up. I could not go through with it. I surely did not wish to hurt Larry, but it was my life, too, and I was not ready to settle down for the rest of my life as a married woman. I told Larry I couldn't go through with it and gave him back his engagement ring. Larry was very hurt and tried desperately to change my mind. My parents and friends all thought I had lost my mind. Larry kept trying to change my mind, and so did my family and friends.

By the end of April, Larry had received his shipping orders and was going to Japan in early July. Larry told me the navy would approve of a wife going along, but not a girlfriend. *Japan! Wow! Japan! Not only is that out of Wisconsin, but it's also out of the country*, I thought.

I had to think about this long and hard. I did love him. The more I thought about it the more I figured everyone must be right, and I must be wrong. There were so many people telling me how lucky I was to have found a guy like Larry and how happy I would be to be married to him. These were my family and friends; they knew what was best for me.

What's the matter with me? I wondered. He wanted to marry me and take me to Japan. Why didn't that all sound like a perfect plan? Larry was so good to me, and I liked being with him. I did love him. But getting married was a huge commitment. *Why can't we be engaged, write to each other, let the relationship grow, and get married when he comes back from Japan?* I asked myself.

I tried to explain my feelings to Larry, but he didn't want to wait. He said we could travel as husband and wife and let the navy take care of everything. Then, when he retired after twenty-five years in the navy, we would buy a house in Yuma, Colorado, and continue to raise our family there. I must admit he painted a rosy picture, although settling down in Yuma, Colorado, did not sound like something I wanted to do. Yuma was a very pleasant place, but Sheboygan was considerably bigger, and the thought of the little town was not so inviting. But, I figured we had twenty-five years to work that out. I agreed to marry him, and the wedding was set for June 27, 1959, a few weeks after I graduated from high school.

My wedding day was very nice. It was a small, but very nice wedding ceremony and reception. Mom and Dad gave us a nice party. It wasn't what I always envisioned my wedding to be, but it was all any of us could afford. The dream of a huge wedding with a fancy gown and a long walk down the isle in a beautiful church was just not meant to be. The dream of a honeymoon in some exotic place was not meant to be, either. Larry said he would make it up to me someday.

Larry was assigned to the ship and had to be there every day. He was not allowed to live off the ship, and I was not allowed to live on the ship, so we spent the greater part of our newly married days apart. Larry told me that I could not go to Japan right away, that he would have to go there first, find out what the procedures were for navy wives, and then send for me. We had been married only seventeen days when Larry left for Japan.

I stayed with Mom and Dad and took a full-time job to save money before I left for Japan. Larry and I wrote to each other often, almost every day.

After three months, I found out I was pregnant and in my letters pressed him harder about when I would be able to join him. Larry and I both were happy about the baby, but Larry could not answer the nagging question of when I would be with him.

Around late September 1959, I had a miscarriage. Although my mom and dad were very supportive, my husband was not there and could not come home. It was an incomplete miscarriage, which means that the fetus died, but wasn't expelled, so I ended up in the hospital for a D and C, a dilation and curettage, which is a procedure in which the doctor scrapes out the uterus. I was crushed and scared and needed my husband for support.

Around Christmas 1959, Larry wrote to me and finally told me the truth. I could not join him in Japan. He did not have enough rank for his wife to come to him, and he admitted that he knew that before we got married. He asked for my understanding. He explained that he loved me and was so afraid our love was not strong enough to endure until he returned from Japan that he had thought we needed to get married before he left.

I was beginning to feel trapped, and my heart was crushed again. I thought life should be different when you got married. How could he have lied to me and built up my hopes like that? Love wasn't supposed to be like that. I only wanted to be near my husband. That was not asking too much. Japan wasn't even important anymore. That we weren't going to be together for what seemed like an eternity was the issue.

I was nineteen years old, married, and still living at home with my parents. I had been pregnant and had had a miscarriage. Now I was being hit by the latest blow—being told by my husband that he had lied to me right from the beginning. I wished I was a little girl again. I didn't like being an adult if that was what it was going to be like.

I guess I kind of rebelled at that stage in my life. I started staying out late in the teen bars. In the late 1950s and early 1960s, there were bars in Wisconsin that only served beer and were open to eighteen-year-olds. These bars were places young adults could hang out, but people still had to be twenty-one to go to regular taverns and bars. It was nice to visit with old school friends and to be able to have a beer if I wanted to.

I also started smoking cigarettes. It just seemed like the thing to do. My mom was angry, and I got a lecture on the health hazards, but Dad smoked, so I figured it wasn't going to kill me. Besides I was a married woman and could do as I pleased. She even tried telling me Larry would be angry with me, too, like that held any water.

The days just seemed to drag by until one day; Dad came home from the doctor's office and told Mom that he had diabetes. Dad and I cried, but Mom just started reading up on how to cook meals for diabetics. She took it in stride and started planning ahead. I wondered if deep down she was crying, too, but wanted to model for us that crying wasn't going to fix a thing. It wasn't the end of the world; after all, he wasn't going to die; he just had to make some changes in his eating habits and lifestyle. I thought to myself, *What a strong person she is. I truly love her for taking charge of this crisis.*

I guess she had to deal with so many illnesses of her own that she just learned how to cope, deal with the circumstances, and move on. But as strong as she seemed at the moment, I was certain I heard her crying later in her bedroom.

When my brother, sister, and I were young, Mom was diagnosed with lupus and myasthenia gravis. She had to give herself an injection every day. I was there one morning when she had to give herself an injection. She said that she wanted me to watch because there might come a day when she wouldn't have the strength to give herself the injection and I might have to do it for her. I said, "Oh no, I could never stick you with a needle." I remember her reply. She said, "If I was going to die without it, you'd do it." She was right! No matter how hard it would have been to do, I would have done it. So many times during my life I have thought of her strength and hoped I could be that strong.

Apart from this news, life seemed to stand still. I wanted to run away and get started on a new life. In February of 1960, my best friend Bonnie Sanville and I decided to make a break for it. We wanted to just leave Sheboygan and get far enough away to be ourselves. We got an apartment in Chicago, moved there, and found jobs. We split the expenses.

Larry was furious with me because he wanted me to stay with Mom and Dad and save money for when he returned. *What the heck? What is he going to do? He's in Japan,* I remember thinking. Mom and Dad were not happy with me either because I was going against my husband's wishes. Yes, there it was again—my husband who was my boss, my legal guardian since I was not twenty-one years old yet. Was I worried? No, I think not.

I had found a good job in Chicago in the main office of a major electric company. My job was to check the mail, match payments to bills, and pass them to the next person who would do the accounting portion of it. Life was fun and new. I was experiencing a whole new way of living.

To tell the truth, I didn't even care what Larry thought. I knew he wouldn't be in the United States again until around the end of July, and by then he would get over it.

My mom was very upset that I had run off like that and lectured me about making a mistake. I was angry with my mom for trying to control my life, and I wrote a letter explaining how I felt, but addressed it only to my dad. The letter I got back from my dad told me I had hurt my mom and if I ever sent another letter addressed only to him, it would be returned unopened.

At the time I guess I did not truly understand how painful it can be for a mother to try to keep her children safe, give them advice, and yet not run their lives. I would later learn about this pain firsthand. What goes around comes around, and I am later paid back for the hurtful things I did and said.

In Chicago eighteen-year-olds could legally go into any tavern or nightclub. Both Bonnie and I were really feeling like adults now. Not only were we not feeling like teenagers, but also we were feeling like we belonged among the adults. I was introduced to a drink called Tom Collins, made with vodka or gin. Both versions tasted like lemonade with a light kick. It sure was better than beer. We weren't out every night, but we certainly did our share of nightclubbing.

Around the early part of May, I started to get nervous about Larry's return in July. This was my husband. We were only married seventeen days before he went away for a year. *Will he be a different person now? I know I am.* I was certainly headstrong and my own person. Life was about to make another turn.

I pleaded with Bonnie to travel to Long Beach, California, with me to be there when Larry's ship came in. I convinced myself that if I had an apartment set up for us he might be happy about that. And if Bonnie was there he couldn't be angry with me in front of my friend, and I wouldn't have to be alone with this stranger who was my husband. At first Bonnie did not want to go because she didn't have the money to travel and she didn't want to interfere in my marriage by being there the first night he was back. I pestered her and offered to pay her train fare. Finally Bonnie agreed, and we started making plans to travel. The train seemed to be the cheapest way to travel, and we would get to see the country, too.

The last week in May 1960, Bonnie and I boarded a train for California. It was the type of train that you could get off at any stop you wanted to and then get back on when you were ready. We had no intentions of getting off before California, but then we read some pamphlets about Albuquerque, New Mexico, on the train. *How exciting! What the heck! Riding horses into the sunset on a ranch for just a couple of days won't hurt. We have the time.* It was an adventure, and I wanted to savor all of it. I was finally out of Wisconsin and on my way to California. No one was telling me what I could or could not do. Who would have believed that? Life was good, yet exciting and scary in a way.

Albuquerque, New Mexico, was not as exciting as the pamphlets said it would be. And, it was expensive. I was afraid to spend too much money since Bonnie and I were both living on the money I had saved from the Navy checks and from the savings account. I knew I had better have some money saved for when Larry got back. Yet, *what will he do, divorce me! I think not,* I convinced myself.

I telephoned my aunt and uncle, Adella and John Upton, who lived in Los Angeles. I asked if they could help us get to Long Beach so that I could get an apartment. My aunt and uncle were very glad to help us out and said we could stay with them for a few days. Bonnie and I got back on the train after just less than a week in Albuquerque and continued on our trip to California.

We arrived in Los Angeles, and my uncle met us at the train station. We went to my aunt and uncle's house. They had a beautiful house, but to tell you the truth we were a little surprised at the iron bars on the windows. It was a nice neighborhood, but a good percentage of the homes there had bars on the windows. I remember thinking to myself, *How awful. People are so afraid of break-ins that they have to put bars on the windows. We don't have to do that in Wisconsin.*

We were awestruck at the sights in Los Angeles. The freeways were awesome and overlapping each other, five or six lanes across, and the buildings were so tall. Nothing like Wisconsin! The weather was warm, and the palm trees were beautiful. There were flowers and fruit trees everywhere.

Bonnie and I stayed in the little summer cottage my aunt and uncle had in the backyard. It was very comfortable. My uncle took Bonnie and I sightseeing the very next day. We went to see the footprints of the stars in the forecourt of Grauman's Chinese Theatre. We saw Beverly Hills and Rodeo Drive. What an exciting place to live, and to think that I had hardly ever been out of Wisconsin. Look at what all I was missing. It was like a new world with different cultures and sights galore, and it was so nice and warm.

The next morning my uncle took us to Long Beach.

Long Beach, at last! We bought a paper and almost immediately found a reasonably priced apartment. It wasn't too far from the docks where the navy ships came in. I was truly glad because I had no idea where we would go if we hadn't found one.

The apartment was small, but that was all right. Bonnie and I were used to small. It was an upper apartment with a terrace that opened to the street in front. The big surprise came a few days later when we found out we had eight United States Marines living downstairs from us! All eight were on the same aircraft carrier in port at Long Beach.

It was hard to believe that it was June already and that Larry would be home in a few short weeks. I was very nervous and worried. I was a married woman who barely knew her husband. I was feeling a bit like a woman in an arranged marriage who didn't have any choice. I did love Larry, but, after all, a whole year had gone by. And what was love? Did I really know what that was supposed to be?

Bonnie and I partied hardy with the guys downstairs. They were fun and cute and all from different states. We drank a lot. My drink was vodka sour or gin and sour.

Our next door neighbors were a pharmacist and his wife. They would check on us once in a while to make sure we were all right. It was kind of nice to have someone around who was older and concerned about us. However, they did not interfere with our lives, and we continued to party.

Around early July, I thought I had the flu. I had such terrible back pain with it that I was miserable. I knew I had to at least get checked out. I managed to get myself to the naval clinic. They took tests and decided I had a case of appendicitis. I had to go back to the clinic to get a shot of antibiotics every day for a week. By the end of that week I was so sick I couldn't eat. Everything was coming up and out. I also had a fever, but refused to go to back to the doctor or even to the base for treatment.

I couldn't be sick now; Larry was coming home in a few days. I had to meet the ship or I knew he would be angry with me. Especially since I had come all the way from Wisconsin and gotten an apartment for us, even though he had asked me to stay home and wait.

Unfortunately, I got sicker. Bonnie was worried about me because I couldn't even stand up without falling down and my fever had gone up to 104 degrees. Bonnie spoke to the pharmacist next door and asked for his help. He checked on me and said I was going to the hospital whether I liked it or not. He asked the guys downstairs to help get me into the car. They placed me on a chair and carried the chair down the flight of stairs and out to the car. I was very upset and crying loudly to please not take me; I had to meet the ship, but I was too weak to fight.

Bonnie and the pharmacist assured me that they would meet the ship and explain to Larry where I was and why I wasn't there. They left for the ship with his picture, his name, and the name of the ship. Neither one of them knew Larry personally.

As they promised, Bonnie and the pharmacist met the ship and told Larry where I was. As it turned out, he had duty that day and wouldn't have been able to come home with me anyway had I been healthy and met him myself. After hearing the news about my condition, Larry found a replacement for his duty station and came to the hospital. The very next day he came to see me again. I was diagnosed with double kidney infection and was hospitalized for a week. The doctor told me I owed my life to the pharmacist because if I had waited any longer before coming to the hospital I might have died. He also explained that the vodka and gin were the source of my illness. Apparently drinking considerable amounts of vodka and gin over such a long time is very bad for the kidneys. I had been drinking that stuff for months and a lot of it.

The doctor also told me to quit smoking. Luckily, being in the hospital for a week with no cigarettes was the first step to quitting anyway, so it was not all that difficult for me.

This may sound strange, but I was glad I was in the hospital for a week because it gave Larry and I time to become reacquainted. And, of course, while I was in the hospital he could not scold me for coming to California. He was very caring and concerned about me. I guess the whole incident was what we needed to reunite as husband and wife.

The doctor ordered complete rest for me and recommended that Larry take me away somewhere quiet. Larry had wanted to take me to Colorado to see his parents, but the doctor suggested I not travel by airplane or train because I was too weak. So, Larry decided he would take some leave and we would go to Palm Springs and just sit in the sunshine by a pool in peace and quiet for a week. We could make plans for where we wanted to live and what we wanted to do next. It turned out to be the honeymoon we had not had when we got married. It was wonderful. I was so glad to have him back with me. I finally remembered why I had married him. I truly loved him.

Bonnie left for Wisconsin while I was still in the hospital. I knew I would miss her, since she was very much a sister to me by then. We had been through so much together. I wondered if she would write, if we would stay in touch.

When Larry and I returned to our apartment, it seemed so empty without Bonnie. Larry didn't like the guys downstairs, so I figured we wouldn't be living there long.

Within two weeks Larry made plans for us to move to federal housing in San Pedro. A lot of navy families were there, and the rent was charged on a sliding scale based on your income so it was very reasonable. We were eligible for a one-bedroom, upstairs apartment that faced the main street and harbor. It was on a corner and had a nice view, so I didn't mind. The walls were very thin, and cockroaches ran everywhere. Sad to say, but everyone got used to them after a while. We would turn on the kitchen light and wait for them to scatter before doing whatever we had gone into the kitchen to do, and we learned to never put dishes on the table without rewashing them first.

Larry and I were finally a family. I cooked and cleaned and took the clothes to the Laundromat. I learned to starch and iron his whites for his summer uniforms. We went to a movie once a month for our only entertainment. There were no more parties. But that was all right. I guess I was partied out anyway.

Life was pretty good, except when Larry had duty on the ship and could not come home nights or weekends. Then it got very lonely. I was bored and watched old movies on television every night. Larry did not want me to walk around without him there because the streets were not exactly safe by the harbor. Lots of homeless, street people wandered around. Some carried wine bottles in paper bags. We didn't have a car and couldn't afford to get one, so I was stuck at home alone.

As this went on, I realized that life was not turning out as I had expected; it was no longer good. I offered to get a job, but Larry refused to let me work. I tried desperately to convince him that I could work on the naval base like some of the other wives, but he just put his foot down and said no. He wanted me to be home when he was in port, not at some job. I guess he didn't like being home alone either. This seemed pretty hypocritical, but I respected his wishes.

Larry began to see my frustration, and he made attempts to introduce me to wives of other shipmates. One of his shipmates had six children and a house that was so filthy I didn't want to step foot in it. But this was a good friend of Larry's so I had no choice. I did have a choice, however, when Larry was not around, so I chose not to visit his friend's wife and kids while the men were out at sea. His wife was a wonderful woman, but I did not approve of the way they lived. She mostly sat at her kitchen table, drank coffee, and smoked cigarettes. The kids did their own thing without any supervision. I did not want to be like that or live like that.

Larry would be gone out to sea for three months, six months, or nine months at a time, and I was so lonely. I bought a kitten to keep me company. He was not happy with the kitten. I guess they were even because the kitten did not particularly like Larry either. When Larry would fall asleep on the couch the kitten would lick the top of his head until it was soaking wet. I never really figured out why, maybe it liked the texture of Larry's short military haircut. I tried to keep it away, but it went back every time. Then Larry would jump up, complaining about his wet head and scaring the kitten who would go hide. Larry wanted me to get rid of the kitten, but I refused. I was not going to be held a prisoner in the apartment without the only company I had when he was gone.

One summer I joined the Navy Officers' Wives' Club, when Larry was out at sea for six months. As I recall there were about twenty women who got together. We would meet once a month to go have lunch somewhere, go sightseeing, or just stay at the officers club to have a meeting, play cards, or discuss projects and group outings. Some of the women would have alcohol, but I didn't.

It was fun. I remember once we all placed a dollar in a pot. The next meeting was to be crazy hat day, and each of us was supposed to make a crazy hat. Then everyone would vote and the winner would get the money. I made my hat out of the neighbors' tinker toys. It was very heavy, but it sure looked unusual. When we gathered again for crazy hat day, it was so much fun. We all laughed at everyone's creations, and, to my surprise, I won the money. I was so happy and couldn't wait to tell Larry. One of the ladies asked to borrow the hat because she was going to be attending a television show at which people wore crazy things to get picked from the audience for prizes. As I recall she was never picked, but I was proud she thought enough of my crazy hat to ask for it.

When Larry came back into port, I told him about the club and the hat and about how much fun I was having with the ladies. After all, it was an officers' club and the ladies were all just that, ladies. Larry told me he did not want me to go and that I had to quit the club. I was very upset because when he was out to sea it was so lonely. Larry argued that he would be home for a stretch now and he wanted me home when he came home. We would discuss the matter again the next time he got orders to go out to sea; otherwise, that discussion was over.

3
And Baby Makes Three

When I found out I was pregnant, both Larry and I were ecstatic. How wonderful—a baby! A little human being would be there to keep me company. That would surely change things and keep me busy. I had to take the bus to the naval base to get prenatal care, and those were wonderful outings for me. I didn't care that it was only a trip to the doctor's office because at least I was out of the apartment. It was like a day of freedom. Sad, but true! I planned for the baby and bought a few things each month. We didn't have much money, but shopping was so much fun. There were such cute little baby things to purchase. I guess by then Larry figured he couldn't keep me locked up in that apartment all the time, and he stopped complaining about my leaving the house.

One night we took the bus to Long Beach to see a movie. Larry got up in the middle of the movie to go to the bathroom. He seemed to be gone a long time. When he finally came back, he said, "Let's go." I was wondering what was wrong because the movie wasn't over. He insisted we leave. Outside he told me he had passed out in the bathroom and had hit his head on the sink on the way down. I saw blood on the top of his head and insisted that we go immediately to the naval clinic on the base. He didn't want to go because he didn't think anything was wrong with him. I told him that nobody passes out without a reason and that he needed to get the cut on his head checked out anyway.

The doctors didn't just check Larry out; they placed him on the naval hospital ship where they kept him for several days so that they could run tests to try to find out why he had passed out.

I later found out that this was not the first time he had passed out; it had happened at least twice before on the ship. I was very concerned about him. I needed him, especially then, when we were about to have a baby.

Larry was released from the hospital, and he told me that the doctors hadn't been able to determine why he had passed out. Over the next few weeks, Larry seemed fine, as if it had never happened. I never received any paperwork telling me of any results, so I had to believe that my husband was telling the truth. I figured that if there was really something wrong, they would have discharged him or at the least would have been watching him closely.

I agreed that the kitten, who was then a cat, had to go. I had heard many ugly stories about cats that had lain down on a baby's face and had suffocated the infant. True or not, I was not going to take a chance like that. We took the cat to the humane society. I hope the cat had a chance at another good home.

In 1961, I was in my ninth month of pregnancy when my twenty-first birthday arrived. Larry took me out to dinner and then we went to his friend's house—yes the one I didn't like—to end the evening with a few bottles of wine—cheap wine. I believe it was called Ripple, and it came in bottles about the size of a small soda bottle. I had a little wine to celebrate my birthday. The next day I was not feeling well. Larry thought it was funny.

Larry was due to go out to sea again for a few months. I was very upset because I didn't want to be alone when our first child was born. However, the navy did not think having a baby was reason enough not to go to sea, so he left.

On October 17, 1961, I went into labor. At least I thought it might be labor: I had such a backache that I couldn't stand or sit. I walked over to my neighbors', because we didn't have a telephone, and asked for their help. They took me to the Fort McArthur Army Hospital in San Pedro.

Yes, I was in labor, they informed me, and our first child was going to be born soon. I was not given any drugs at all, but I fell asleep during the labor pains. I thought to myself, *what are all these women complaining about? Childbirth is a snap. I will have many children.*

The labor took about 12 hours and I was awake for the birth. Our daughter Diana Lynn was born. She was beautiful and so tiny. I named her Diana Lynn after a movie star whom I admired in the old movies I always watched. The movie star was beautiful in every way. She had a beautiful smile and always played the kind and charming roles. I hoped my Diana Lynn would be just like that. The hospital sent a telegram to Larry on the ship to let him know that he was now a father and had a little girl.

The nurses in the hospital took care of Diana Lynn and let me rest. When it was time to take her home, I was a little scared. I had this little person to care for and knew nothing about being a mother. As a teenager I had babysitting jobs, but never for one so young and so small. I had no clue what to do with her.

The same neighbors that took me to the hospital picked us up. I must admit I was kind of glad to be going home to our apartment, but then Larry was still at sea and would not be back for a few days yet. I would have to be the only caretaker for our new daughter.

What kind of mother will I be? Am I old enough for this responsibility? Will Larry be a good father, being gone all the time? I calmed my fears by thinking about the other families who managed in federal housing, figuring that we would, too.

The hospital gave me a gift basket of baby shampoo, baby powder, baby oil, baby lotion, Vaseline, and various other products. It was a nice gift. The next day, I gave Diana a bath for the first time; boy, was she slippery. But it went all right, and I was proud of myself for getting through the first bath. I took the basket of products and put a little of each product on her, as I thought that was why they gave it to me. She needed all that stuff. I learned to boil the bottles and make the formula in batches. It seemed she didn't sleep much. She cried, and I would run to pick her up. I didn't want to upset her; besides, I had to make sure she was not sick or something. I carried her around a lot.

Larry was very pleased with and proud of his little princess. However, he refused to change her diapers; he said it was my job. He telephoned my parents and his parents with the news.

I didn't know it at the time, but my mom was gravely ill and in the hospital fighting for her life when Diana was born. They didn't want to tell me because they knew I couldn't come home anyway and didn't want to alarm me while I was that close to delivery. The story they told me was that when my mom found out she was a grandmother for the first time, she told the doctors she was going to fight to stay alive to see her new grandchild. I wonder if that news didn't truly save her life. The doctors told my dad a few days later that my mom had made a miraculous recovery.

One day my aunt and uncle from Los Angeles came to visit. Diana had messed in her diaper, and my aunt barked out instructions to go get a washcloth. I followed her orders and, unfortunately, forgot to make it a warm washcloth. She proceeded to give me a lecture on washing a baby's behind with a cold washcloth. That didn't particularly upset me because I was still learning, but I sure was feeling inadequate. I guess I was just glad she was there, because my mom could not be. It was a pleasant visit, and she explained what all the things in the gift basket were for, the oil, powder, lotion, and so forth. We both had a good laugh when I told her I was putting a little of everything in the basket on Diana.

Larry was very much navy-oriented and took his job on the ship seriously. When I would complain because he got orders to go out to sea again, he would tell me, "The United States Navy was number one, family was number two, and if the navy had wanted me to have a family they would have issued it with the seabag." It was his choice to have a family, and I needed to adjust. Being a navy wife was not what I had expected it to be. Maybe I was not adult enough to understand this lifestyle. I was, however, very proud of him for serving our country.

I began to adjust because I had Diana to keep me company, and she was such a joy. It was like make-believe and playing with a doll, only this doll needed food, diaper changes, and, most of all, my love and attention.

I was, what I considered to be, a good homemaker. I would iron dresses and wear aprons. One incident in particular comes to mind when I think about how I tried so hard to be the good wife and mother. Larry had been out to sea for a couple of weeks. I was glad he was coming home and wanted everything to be just right. I cleaned the house thoroughly. I had my pink checkered dress ironed and a clean apron ironed. I took a bath, fixed my hair, and made sure that Diana was fresh and clean and in a cute little pink dress. I had made a special pot roast and had the table set just right. When Larry came in he was happy to be home but seemed very tired. Apparently he had been on duty much of the last day before coming into port, and it was a long trip. He took off his dress uniform and carefully hung it up while I went to get the dinner on the table. When he was about to put his shoes in the bedroom closet I heard him say something. I went to the bedroom to see what it was, and he lashed out at me for not cleaning and mopping the closet floor. He did not wish to put his polished uniform shoes in a dirty closet and wanted to know why didn't I have it clean, since I had "all the time in the world" to get the house cleaned before he came home.

I broke into tears because I had tried so hard to make his homecoming a pleasant one. *I never thought about the closet. Who would?* Dinner was a quiet one and I no longer cared. I just went through the motions. Larry knew he had upset me and was all apologies. He said that he was just tired and that I should take it for that and nothing more. He said he could see that everything else was clean and in order and he did appreciate all the trouble I had gone through to make a nice homecoming for him.

Larry wanted me to know how sorry he was, so he offered to get the neighbor to babysit for us the next night while we went to a movie. I thought that was a nice gesture and agreed that it would be nice for both of us to be alone together away from the apartment.

We stopped at a local bar after the movie and had a few drinks. It didn't take much to get me loaded since I had not had any alcohol for a long time. When we got home I had to boil the baby bottles and make the formula. Both Larry and I fell asleep while the bottles were boiling. When I woke up it was so hard to breathe in there I quickly woke Larry and opened some windows. The water had boiled off, and the baby bottles, caps, and nipples had melted in the pot. We took precautions to cover Diana so the smoke and cold from the windows wouldn't get to her, and we went to the bottom of the steps until the smoke had cleared some. I will never forget how scared I was. We could have burned the apartment down, maybe even lost Diana. The fumes were terribly strong, but I didn't want to take Diana outside. Would she get sick? Then I had to give her formula in a small juice bottle. All the bottles had melted so I had no other choice. We couldn't go shopping at two o'clock in the morning. The smell made me nauseous. Or, was it the combination of alcohol and fear that made me sick? What was supposed to be a nice quiet night out turned into a disaster.

The next day we had to go buy all new baby bottles, caps, and nipples. I also reconsidered the need to boil everything. *Why wouldn't it be good enough to just wash it in hot soapy water and use the tongs to hold the bottle and rinse it under hot water? That should kill any lurking germs.* From then on I stopped boiling the bottles.

When Diana was about ten months old, I noticed she was having trouble standing, and even though I worked with her on learning to walk, she would not. She would crawl but not walk. I decided to take her to the naval clinic to get her checked out. The doctors didn't know why she wouldn't walk, but they noticed that her legs appeared to be crooked. The only suggestion they had was to break both her legs and reset them. But, they said, even then there was no guarantee she would walk. I was repulsed by their suggestion. No one was going to break her legs, and I told them that the only way they could was over my dead body. I decided that I would keep working with her and that if that didn't help I would take her to a bone specialist.

4

It's a Boy

When Diana was a little over a year old, I found out that I was pregnant again. And, almost immediately after that Larry received orders to go overseas. This time it would be for nine months to a year. Obviously I was extremely upset about that. Once again, there I was expecting a baby without my husband by my side. *How can the navy be so important? How come I'm the one always feeling left behind to cope?* I thought.

Larry was concerned about my frustration and decided it would be best for me to go home to stay with my family in Wisconsin. The plan was that I would have the baby in Wisconsin and when he got back from overseas he would come and get us all and we would travel back to California together. Going back to Wisconsin sounded good to me. At least I wouldn't be alone.

Diana and I flew back to Wisconsin to live with my grandmother who, as I mentioned before, lived three houses north of my parent's house. Everyone was very happy to have the first grandchild at home. I loved my mom, dad, grandmother, sister, and brother. It was very nice being home.

I got to see some of my old friends, and that was nice, too. Tom McCue and his wife Liz became very good friends of mine. Liz was a good homemaker, and I thought she and Tom made a good couple. They had a little girl Susan about the same age as Diana. Tom would come and get me and Diana and take us to their house in Sheboygan Falls. Diana and I would spend most of the day with Liz and Susan. Liz and I played cards, and the girls played with toys; it was just a really good time. I often thought about how lucky I was not being stuck in that apartment in San Pedro without Larry.

My mom and I got to be friends again, and she helped me a lot with Diana. We spoke about my mom's concerns about Diana not walking. She would stand, but she still would not take a step. Mom recommended a good doctor at the Sheboygan Clinic.

I made an appointment. When I saw the doctor, I told him about the Navy doctors' recommendation that both her legs be broken. He was very surprised that they even suggested it. After careful examination the doctor told me that Diana had a mild case of cerebral palsy, but that with stretching treatments and therapy, she should be walking in no time. He went on to explain that it was very important to keep those muscles loose because, in some cases, the child ends up in a wheelchair. I was so upset I immediately went home and cried to my mom. What would I do? Mom immediately took charge, made me stop crying, and started a plan for treatments.

She has always said that in the wake of crisis you must take charge and if you must fall apart, do it later. She was so wise. Why was I so mean to her when I was a young adult! I will be trying to make it up to her until my last days on this earth.

After a couple of weeks, Diana was walking. I was so pleased with her progress. Every night Diana and I would get on the floor and would work on her stretching exercises. She didn't like it much because it hurt, but I knew she would understand and thank me when she was an adult. I tried to make the trips to the therapist a fun day out for the two of us, but I always knew it would be painful for her and felt guilty for making her suffer. My mom would always have to reassure me that it was best for Diana and that even though it was painful for her, it was a necessity.

Often I thought about Larry. Where was Diana's father through all of this? Why wasn't he helping his family when they needed him? Why did he always have to be gone? But that was a silly question. I had to remember that we were not number one; the navy held that honor. I may be perceived as a whiner, but unless you had to live that way, it is hard to understand.

Diana and I survived the next few months, and my due date was fast approaching. We set up a baby crib in the area Diana and I called our bedroom. I could see she was anxious to find out what I was going to put in that crib. I was so big and tired. I felt like I was going to deliver a baby elephant. Larry and I wrote to each other and picked out names. If the baby was a boy, we would name him Leary after Larry's dad. If it was a girl, we would name her Loretta. I liked country music, and there was a country music singer whose name was Loretta. I thought the name sounded magical.

On June 3, 1963, I went into labor. Mom took me to the hospital in Sheboygan. I was so glad she was there but still missed my husband. I almost hated the navy for keeping us apart, especially when I needed him most.

This labor was quite a change from Diana's birth. Instead of falling asleep during labor pains like I did with her, I endured hours of excruciating labor pains. The baby did not want to come out and kept turning its head. I thought I was going to die. Finally, with help from the doctor, our son Leary Arthur was born. Dad contacted the Red Cross and they sent a message to Larry on the ship to tell him that he had a baby boy.

Diana loved her little brother; she would stand for what seemed like hours just staring at him in the crib. Once she stuck her little arm in the crib and tried to poke him in the eye to see if he would open it, but I caught her just in time. I guess she didn't think he was real.

My grandmother told me Diana was a handful while I was in the hospital. She would take the little hair barrettes out of her hair and try to throw them down the heat registers. Grandmother said she would have to run after her, but Diana was too quick. The barrettes would melt and stink. Diana didn't understand. Instead, she thought it was a game called "beat great-grandma to the heat register," and she would laugh and giggle. My grandmother would pat her on the bottom a couple of times, but the light spanking didn't faze her. We had to just stop using hair barrettes, and then the game was over.

Diana and I still worked on her leg-stretching exercises, and at night she had to sleep with a brace on her shoes to keep her feet pointed outward. She didn't like it much but grew accustomed to it after awhile. Eventually she could even crawl around with them on, and then I resigned myself to the fact that she was adjusting to wearing them.

5

Back to California

When Leary was ten days old my husband was back from overseas and was there in Sheboygan to pick us up as he had promised. I was very glad he was there, yet I was sad because his arrival meant we would be leaving Wisconsin to return to California and to navy life.

Larry bought a car and planned to drive us back to California because, as he said, it would be cheaper in the long run and we had the time before he had to report back to his ship. We packed everything we owned, which was not much, into the car and away we went.

According to Larry we had to drive directly to California, with no time to stop in Yuma, Colorado, because he wanted to be able to get us situated in the federal housing where we would set up house again. It was the same housing development we were in before—good old San Pedro, the lonely life and the cockroaches. I couldn't wait. I held out hope that this time things would be different.

When we arrived there was a two-bedroom apartment waiting for us. It was actually just two blocks from where we had lived before. It seemed like the same people were there, but this time we had different neighbors.

The apartment wasn't all that bad. It had a bathroom and two bedrooms upstairs and a kitchen and living room downstairs. Our back door opened into a courtyard where the children could play. However, the walls were very thin, and we could hear the neighbor's coffee pot perking in the morning. If they had a telephone call at night, we could hear the whole conversation. But our neighbors on both sides were nice and welcomed us to the neighborhood.

I became very close friends with the family on the right side of us. They were from Texas. Beatrice Gonzales, the mother of the household, had three children—two girls and a boy. She was a kind person who worked hard. Beatrice ironed everything from sheets to shorts. I hated ironing and could never understand why she liked to do it. Her husband was gone a lot, too, but she didn't seem to mind. I guess she had been a navy wife for so long it seemed like the way to live.

Time passed, and it seemed to me that Larry was out to sea more than in. But I kept busy with the two children and all the housework.

One time when Larry was out to sea, the washing machine broke down. I took the top of the machine off and found that a rubber thing had broken. I took the rubber piece to an appliance repair shop and found out that the piece was called a snubber ring. I bought a new one and replaced it. Then I put the machine top back on and was very proud to say I had repaired it. In those days we had to make due. We didn't have the money to call a repairman, and we had to make every effort to repair things by ourselves to save money. I even took tubes out of my TV set and replaced them to keep the TV going.

As time went by I started to get very depressed. I hated the navy and the navy life. What good was it? The father, the head of the household, was hardly ever home and that was evident by the way some people lived. They didn't care much either. Everyone just seemed to plug along making life as bearable as they could, just waiting for the father and beloved husband to return home. There was nothing for me to entertain myself with except television, but that got old, too. I had the children, but that wasn't enough. I missed having an adult around to sit and talk with in the evening when the children were in bed.

I had become close friends with Bob and Marian Taylor who lived two apartments down from us. They were older than us but were very nice and friendly. Larry liked them, too. Often we would get together, play cards, and just talk. Marian became like a sister to me. We became very close.

One day Bob received word that he was being transferred to Lemoore Naval Air Base just north of Hanford, California, and they would soon be moving.

I was losing some close friends, but that was what service life was like. You made friends, and then they were transferred or you were transferred. That's why you would try not to get too close to people, military life was not stable. Friends would regularly leave.

My depression got out of hand and became more evident. Larry suggested I go to the naval clinic to talk to a doctor. I agreed. Whether or not I thought it would help, I was just glad to get out of the house by myself for a few hours. The doctor seemed to think my depression could be alleviated with the help of Valium. He told me to take three tablets a day but no more than that. He also recommended that I visit my neighbors when I got depressed to try to shake the feelings. But I felt that there wasn't anything wrong with me; it was the navy life that was making me nuts. *I am always alone. Why do I always have to be alone*! I asked myself.

Bob and Marian had been gone about six months when Larry decided we should go visit them at their place in Hanford. He had spoken to them on the telephone, and they had said they would be delighted to have us as houseguests. It was a four-hour drive, but it was through the mountains and was beautiful.

It was so peaceful in Hanford. I loved it there. I wished we could live there, too. I made up my mind, if I ever got the chance, I would try to talk Larry into moving to Hanford when he got out of the service. Words can barely express how much Hanford felt like home. I had an inner peace there. However, it was just a visit and we had to go back to San Pedro.

The Valium helped with my depression a little bit, but sometimes I still felt like everything was just hopeless. Life was a drag. It seemed like I just trudged through each day just to get it over with. *Is this what life is all about? Is this what it is supposed to be?* I asked myself.

One day it all finally got the better of me. I had supper on the stove and was ironing. The children were playing upstairs, and I knew Larry would be home soon. I was crying and kept telling myself I should knock on the wall for Beatrice to come over, but I never did that. Instead, I walked over to the sink and swallowed the whole bottle of Valium pills. I don't know how many pills were in the bottle, but it was a handful. I took them all! It was not something I planned. I didn't even think about it; it just happened.

I knew the children would be all right because Larry would be home soon. I just wanted to escape. I just wanted to sleep. I then went upstairs and hid the bottle. To this day I do not know why I did that. I came back downstairs, turned off the iron, and removed it from the ironing board so no one would get burned. Then I sat at the kitchen table with my head in my hands and tried desperately to fall asleep.

Larry came home and found potatoes boiling on the stove and his wife incoherent. He asked Beatrice to take the children, and then he put me in the car and started to drive me to the clinic. Every time he stopped at a stop sign I tried to jump out.

At the clinic they pumped my stomach to get the pills out of my system. I don't remember how long I was there, but I do remember talking to the doctor who said he would write up the incident as a nervous breakdown instead of an attempted suicide, but only if I promised to get professional help. I agreed and immediately set up an appointment with a navy psychiatrist.

The navy had won again. I was totally convinced that the navy was at fault. They had brainwashed my husband into believing that the navy came first and his family came second. We were not his first priority. My life was empty because the navy was more important than I was. And now, I had to see a doctor, a naval doctor. *What am I going to tell him? It's all the navy's fault? How far is that going to get me?* I wondered. I had convinced myself that I would just go through the motions to make everybody happy and when I was ready I would just stop going. After all, it was Larry who had the problem, not me. It was Larry who said if the navy wanted him to have a family they would have packed it with the seabag. I just wanted a normal family life—like my mom and dad had. They were home every night with their children, not out at sea or, worse yet, overseas.

They no longer gave me Valium. I guess it was because they felt I couldn't be trusted, and perhaps they were right. I kept my appointments with the naval psychiatrist, and I suppose in the long run it did me some good. However I don't remember the sessions, I only remember going to them. By that time, I was resigned to the fact that this was my life and the life of my family. My alternative was divorce, and I would never even have considered that option.

I felt bad when I thought about Diana and Leary. *They are so innocent, and I am not being fair to them. They need to be with their father whenever they can. Who am I to be such a selfish person?* I had only been thinking of myself, not them. Shame on me! I decided it would never happen again; I would always be there for them no matter what. After that, things seemed to improve. Again I was the faithful wife waiting at home, cleaning the house, and taking care of the children. I kept busy with the cooking, sewing, and ironing. It wasn't a bad life, except when Larry was gone. When I started to get depressed about that I told myself, *So what? Others are in the same boat, and they can cope.* I often thought of my mom and asked myself how she would've coped if she were in my shoes.

Larry thought that maybe things would be better if he got me out of federal housing and into a rented house in San Pedro, so we moved into this cute little red house up on a hill. It was really nice, and it did make a difference because it seemed more like a home of our own.

A few months later, we got the news that Larry's dad was very sick and in the hospital. Larry took leave and traveled to Colorado to be by his side. Larry didn't think we should travel with him because he didn't know just how ill his dad really was and we couldn't really afford the trip for everyone. We had used our savings on moving expenses.

When Larry arrived, his dad was very disappointed that we did not come with him. He had wanted to see his namesake, his grandson Leary. Larry called home and requested we come to Colorado. So Diana, Leary, and I boarded a train to Colorado to be with Larry and his family. We arrived too late; his dad had already died. It had been cancer. We stayed for the funeral and then traveled together by train back to San Pedro. It was very sad; Larry really loved his dad. It made me think about my parents, too. I wondered how long they would live and whether or not I would be able to be there for them when their time came.

I don't want to give everyone the impression that my life was a living hell because it was not. I just simply did not like being without my husband so often.

We had many good times when he was home and occasionally we would make a picnic basket and take Diana and Leary to the park where we would spend the day as a family. It was wonderful. Larry was good to the children. When he was home he was a good father and husband.

6

Heart Trouble

In 1965, I was pregnant again. I had often thought before I found out I was pregnant again, that we should stop with two children; we had a girl and a boy. But, I was not unhappy with the pregnancy, and Larry was home a lot more. Life was pretty good. We actually seemed like a normal family for a while.

Around Christmas Larry's mom asked to come live with us. She was lonely in Colorado after Larry's dad died. Also, Larry's sister, Elaine, was in the United States Marines and gone all the time, too. Larry convinced me it would be good for the children and it would be good for me, too, with him out to sea all the time. He also convinced me it would be a big help having her there to take care of Diana and Leary when I had the baby. Even though the little red house was small, we would put another bed in the children's bedroom and made the best of it.

I liked Helen, and we became very good friends. At first it seemed so nice to have her there, but as time went by, it seemed more and more like she was trying to come between Larry and I. Larry said her cooking was better than mine, and of course Larry would side with his mom if I said anything wasn't right. When I was cooking she would be right behind me telling me how to do it better. At first I tried to learn from it, but after a while it wore on my nerves.

I often thought, *Is it my imagination? Am I looking for trouble or is she truly interfering with our lives?* Sometimes she would give me money, just a few dollars, and say don't tell Larry—this is just for you. Then, a few days later she would go to Larry and tell him that she had given it to me. Larry would be upset that I hadn't mentioned how nice his mother was being to me and want to know why I was hiding it. Other times, it was just the opposite; she would give money to Larry and tell him not to tell me, that it was just for him to spend, and then a few days later, she would tell me she gave it to him. The stress was pulling us apart, and we argued a lot.

One night the arguing got so bad I told Larry I was going to leave if he didn't do something about our living situation. I guess I was right in his face because he was so angry with me he gave me a shove. I lost my balance and fell stomach first into a chair. I was so scared because it was very close to my due date. Larry was scared, too, because he realized it never should have gone that far. I know he never meant to hurt me or the baby. As it turned out the baby and I were both fine. Thank God!

Obviously, the living arrangement was not working, so we decided to do something about it. Larry placed our names on the Long Beach Naval Housing waiting list. It was newly built housing, so it would be a pleasant change from the federal housing we were in before. We had a good chance to get in soon. Helen resigned herself to the fact she would have to find an apartment of her own and get a job because she would not be able to move into the naval housing with us. I truly hated for that to happen, but I didn't think my marriage could last the way things had been going.

In early April, Helen moved out and into her own place. Life seemed to settle down, and Helen would stop by to visit at least once a week. She loved being with her grandchildren. We started getting along again, too. The children loved to see their grandmother, and I was glad we could repair the relationship.

As my due date drew near, again Larry received orders to go out to sea. I was not happy, to say the least, and often wondered if the navy did it on purpose or, worse yet, Larry volunteered. Neither was true, of course; it was just plain rotten timing. Once again what choice did I have? This was going to be the third child I had to deliver alone.

That was it, no more. I promised myself I would never do it again and I would use whatever birth control methods necessary to make certain. I thought, *A woman needs her husband by her side when she is in labor and delivery. And with military life that is never a certainty.*

One good thing was that this time I was going to have the baby at a regular hospital in San Pedro. I don't remember why. I guess it was because Larry had a higher rank of service than when Leary was born, so this time we could choose to go where we wanted to go.

On May 25, 1966, I went into labor and went by cab to the hospital. Helen stayed with the children at the little red house. I delivered another beautiful baby boy, alone. The delivery was not a difficult one but was not as easy as Diana. We named him Michael Larry. Of course, Larry was out at sea, but he was due back the next day. I considered myself lucky because he was due to be home when I got there.

Michael was two weeks old when we received word that we could move into the naval housing in Long Beach. It was a nice place. We had two big bedrooms and a bathroom upstairs and a nice-sized living room and kitchen downstairs. There was only one way in and out of the house and that was through a gated backyard that had a patio. The fence was high enough that we could not see over it. We were on the corner, and an officer's wife and her two teenaged daughters lived next door. *This is all right; I could like this place*, I thought. It was newly built, so I didn't have to fight the cockroaches every day.

Moving right after I had given birth was not an easy task, but Larry was very helpful. I just did a little unpacking every day and did what I could to make the house our new home. Larry was home most nights, and we were a family again. I tried not to get too happy or comfortable because every day there was a chance he would come home and say he was shipping out again.

Michael didn't seem to be really healthy and was having a hard time drinking his formula, so I took him to the naval clinic. The doctors gave me nose drops to give him and a suction bulb to clean his nose out with. They thought he just had nasal congestion. I hated using that suction bulb; it seemed to have such a strong pull that I was afraid it was hurting more than helping. Michael surely didn't like it either; he would pull away or cry every time I tried to use it. The nose drops did not help, either.

Then Michael developed diarrhea, too. Again we went to the clinic, and again they gave me more nose drops, as well as some eardrops and antibiotics. Again they said he had nasal congestion and, perhaps, now the flu as well.

I knew there was something terribly wrong. Michael did not improve, and it was scaring me. He started vomiting, still had diarrhea, and was not eating properly. He was getting weaker and weaker.

I took him back to the naval clinic again and spoke sternly to the doctor. I told him that I was not a neurotic mother and that I could tell when something was not right with my child. I told him to check Michael over carefully because something was definitely wrong with him, and it was not just nasal congestion. The doctor agreed to have two other doctors take a closer look at Michael. They asked me to wait in the waiting room. I was very nervous that they had taken my child, but after all, they were doctors and perhaps my being so upset was not helping.

When they called me back in the room with Michael, they told me that one of the doctors had noticed that the left side of his chest was slightly enlarged and had recommended Michael be taken to a Long Beach hospital for a full examination. I immediately took him there to get checked out.

At the hospital they decided to admit Michael so they could run some tests on him. They said I should go home because there was nothing more I could do until the test results came back. I went home and cried on Larry's shoulder. I was terribly worried about our newborn son. *Why is this happening! Is it something I did while I was carrying him?* I wondered.

At around midnight that night, we received a telephone call from the hospital. They said that Michael's heart had stopped beating, but they were able to resuscitate him. I sat there in shock from the news. If I had not done what I did, Michael would have been home with us that night and he may have died. *Oh, my God, what would I have done! What if our son would have died when Larry was out to sea*? I thought. I would have hated Larry for that—that we didn't have a normal family life. I would have hated the navy for making us live that way.

Larry and I left Diana and Leary in Helen's care and rushed to the hospital together. *What now?* I thought. *Is this problem from the fall into the chair I had had just before his birth? Is it my fault? Is it Larry's fault for pushing me and causing the fall?* So many things raced through my mind.

When we arrived at the hospital, the doctors had Michael ready to be transferred by ambulance to UCLA Hospital in Los Angeles. They told us that the Long Beach hospital was not equipped to handle heart problems for someone so young. Michael was only three months old. They told us that he might have to have surgery and that they could not do it.

I rode with Michael in the ambulance to UCLA Hospital, and Larry followed in the car. I was so afraid Michael would die before we got there. The trip seemed very fast. All I remember is praying to God to save our child. The crew seemed concerned, too, because they did not even have an oxygen mask small enough for his little face and he appeared to be struggling to get the mask off, all the way there.

When we arrived at the hospital they whisked Michael away and left me standing there to fill out paperwork. I guess I knew it had to be done, but I wanted to be with my son. After I was done with the paperwork, someone told me where I could wait for news and for my husband.

When Larry arrived I was crying and praying. We had to talk. I told Larry that if the fall I had taken into the chair caused this health problem for Michael, I was going to take the children and leave him. I would go back to Wisconsin and make a good home life for the children. I would not stay in an abusive relationship.

The doctor came out and told us Michael had a rare heart disease. Michael had five chambers in his heart instead of the normal four. It was called cor triatriatum. Since Michael was so sick and unstable, they would need to go into surgery as soon as possible. They would use an instrument to try to cut the one chamber open enough to let the blood pump through. They told us his chances of survival were fifty-fifty.

I cried and cried. What would I have done had this happened when Larry was off playing sailor with the navy! Larry and I both were relieved it was not caused by the fall I had taken, but what would change now. Nothing! The navy was still number one, and the family was number two.

My prayers were heard and answered; Michael made it through the surgery but was still in critical condition. Somehow I knew he would be all right now.

Over the next few days he began to improve, and the doctors were happy with his progress. I was there every day hoping to take my son home.

Then, just after a week later, Michael's progress started to deteriorate. He was losing the battle and becoming weak. The doctor told us open heart surgery was needed to try to repair the heart. He also told us that no baby his age had ever survived open heart surgery. But, without the surgery he would certainly die. They needed our consent, and we gave it.

Those were some of the longest hours of my life. *Is he going to be tough enough to pull through this? After all he pulled through the initial surgery*, I thought. I spent most of the waiting time in the chapel praying for my son to have the strength to get through this.

God heard me; Michael not only survived the surgery but also was fighting for his life with all his might. The doctor had to put a sign on his bed asking people to leave him alone unless absolutely necessary for his care because he was a miracle and everyone wanted to examine him. The doctors published an article about Michael in the *Journal of the American Medical Association* (JAMA) because he was now the youngest child to live through open heart surgery. I was so grateful to God for answering my prayers and saving our son.

Michael was four months old when he was released from the hospital. The only thing holding his chest together was four little bandages. I was petrified. My baby was four months old—he needed me to hold him, care for him, and love him. He was my son, but I was afraid of him.

Michael needed to take digitalis. It was a heart medicine administered with an eyedropper. I had to check his pulse every evening at bedtime and give him the amount of digitalis needed per his pulse. If I did not give him enough, he would die. If I gave him too much, he would die. Needless to say, this put unimaginable stress on me. I also feared I might not handle him correctly. *Could the chest cavity open up like a normal cut might?* Believe me I was not prepared for this, and I was so afraid I would do something to hurt my son. Many nights when Larry was on duty and not home, I sat on the floor by Michael's crib and prayed and cried silently.

7
Military Funeral

Then, just when I thought that things couldn't get much worse, Larry came home and said that he'd received orders to go to Vietnam. I was very angry and said "No, not this time!" I needed him home; Michael needed him home; and he was not to go. I knew there was a hardship clause of some kind that he could use to stay home with us, and he had to ask for it. I begged, pleaded, and cried. But, Larry said no that it was his turn to go and he was going. He stood firm; I had no say in the matter. He reminded me again that if the navy had wanted him to have a family they would have packed it with the seabag. It was the middle of September, and he was going to leave on the first week in October—a few days after my twenty-sixth birthday!

The navy called him to duty, and he had to go. To this day I do not understand his thinking and why he had this overpowering need to place the navy before his family. Maybe he was scared, too, and decided this was his way to handle it—just leave.

The next couple of weeks were a haze for me. I could not believe Larry was going to leave us. Especially at that time!

During the week before he left, Larry made sure all the life insurance papers were in order. I, on the other hand, did not even want to discuss it since nothing was going to happen to him and the thought was morbid.

He made me promise that if anything happened to him that I would not change Leary and Michael's last name because he wanted them to carry on the Allen namesake. He was his parents' only son, and it was very important to him that I promise. I had to promise out loud, word for word. It was a promise I did not hesitate to make, but one I never thought I would actually have to keep. I didn't think it was an unreasonable request, and Larry knew if I promised, I would keep that promise no matter what.

Larry decided to leave his wedding ring at home. He said it was because he had heard that when the Vietnamese captured American servicemen, they would torture them more if they knew they were married. I guess I had trouble with that, but I gave up trying to tell him anything at that point. I was angry and hurt and had disconnected myself from him.

The morning he had to leave, Larry requested that I not see him off at the ship like other wives did. He said it was too hard on everyone. He preferred to just leave the house for work like any other day; however, he cried when he said goodbye. For some unknown reason I did not. Usually it was the other way around; I cried, and he did not. But this time I felt calm, like everything would be all right. I don't know why I felt that way, but I remember it well.

The days seemed to move slowly, and I was still afraid of Michael. Many nights I would sit on the floor by his crib and cry silently because I was afraid I might misread his pulse and not give him the correct dosage of digitalis. Sometimes I asked the neighbor to come over and double-check my pulse readings just to make sure. But Michael was a trooper and kept fighting to get stronger.

Larry and I wrote to each other. It seemed like he was emotionally distant, and his letters sounded lonely. A few weeks before Christmas I decided to buy something special for him from his family, so I went shopping. I bought two identical, inexpensive tape players. The tape recorders used small cassettes, and I figured we could mail cassettes back and forth with recorded letters. I thought this was a really nice idea because then the children and I could hear Larry's voice and it would comfort us. The tape players were light blue, and I remember them well. The children and I spoke into the microphone and made a nice Christmas tape for him. Then I mailed his package to him.

Two days after Christmas I received a tape from him. He told us how happy he was to receive our gift. It was so nice to hear his voice, and the children wanted me to play it over and over again. On the tape Larry asked me to mail him his wedding ring and said he was sorry he had left it behind. He said he would take his chances with the Vietnamese. He spoke to the children about being good kids for Mom and said that he hoped the time would go by quickly and he would be home again soon. He also said he had just mailed an envelope to us, which included letters for each of the kids. The children and I sat down and recorded an answer. Knowing that there was a lot of heavy mail during the Christmas season, I rushed our package to the post office in too much of a hurry to think to include the wedding ring.

Two days before New Year's Eve, Michael developed double pneumonia and was hospitalized. I was beginning to think I couldn't take anymore. My husband was gone; Michael was extra sick; and there I was alone again. The doctors told me that Michael's lungs had not developed completely because of the heart problems he had and that pneumonia was for him particularly serious. I knew Larry should have stayed home; I just knew it.

New Year's Eve was just another lonely night for me, and I went to bed early. On New Year's Day, 1967, at approximately 10:00 AM, two naval officers knocked on my door. They were dressed in officers' best and appeared polished and shined. They spoke softly when they told me the navy had deep regrets, but my husband Larry was dead. He had been pronounced dead that morning on January 2, 1967, since Vietnam was a day ahead of us. He had died on the Song

Soi Rai in Nha Be, South Vietnam, and the cause of death was drowning. Their explanation was that he had fallen overboard and drowned.

I thought he had probably blacked out again and then fallen overboard, but they did not say that. I guess I was trying to find a rationalization for the whole thing. After all, Larry was an excellent swimmer. I was stunned and couldn't speak. There were so many questions I should have asked, but I was in shock.

The officers explained that I would be receiving a telegram later that day from the United States Navy stating the fact that Larry was dead. It was protocol to inform me beforehand, since they did not want me to receive the telegram without having told me first that it was coming.

They said that the next day an officer would be assigned to help me with any funeral arrangements I needed to make. They also said they had told Larry's mom, Helen, and that she was on her way to be with me and the children.

I had seen war movies in which they depict officers showing up at the door to tell a mother she had lost her son or a wife she had lost her husband, and it was exactly as I had seen it. I felt that it was a bad dream, that it could not be true.

I was in shock and disbelief. I cried out loudly, and the children cried. Helen arrived and we all cried together. I remember thinking, *What now? I am a widow at twenty-six with three children, one of whom is in the hospital with a life-threatening illness. How can I manage all this! No, this cannot be happening to us.* We had only had seven years of married life together.

I hadn't even had a chance to send him his wedding ring, and now it was too late. I was never so alone in my whole life. I prayed for help. I needed help not only to get through the funeral but also to guide me to do what I needed to do for the children.

I was oblivious to the neighbors who all stopped by to offer their condolences. Later, I learned that everyone had frozen in their tracks when they saw the officers arrive at the naval complex because everyone knew the scenario and knew why the officers were there; they just didn't know which family was going to receive the bad news.

Helen and I worked out the details and decided Larry should have a military funeral and be buried in Yuma, Colorado, next to his father. It would take a week before the body could be flown back to the United States, so we had time to make arrangements. I did not have a lot of money and had no clothes for a funeral. It was winter, so I needed a dress coat, too. Everything was a blur. I sure didn't want to shop.

I had just lost my husband and wondered if I would lose my son, too. Again I prayed to God to help Michael get better and to please help me get through the whole ordeal. I thought of my mom and how she would handle it. So I took a deep breathe and said, "With God's help I can get through this; just please only one day at a time; give me strength. My children need me now more than ever." It was not the time to give up. I had to be strong for them.

Helen and I agreed that Diana, who had just turned five in October, and Leary, who was just three, were too young to understand a funeral and would stay home with the neighbors. Michael, who was only seven months old, was still in the hospital fighting for his life and could not travel anyway. I'm still not sure whether or not that was the right thing to do since Larry was their dad. And maybe it was selfish of me, but I was so numb and unable to cope with the whole idea of burying my husband that I didn't think I could handle small children on the long trip. It would be tough enough to get through it myself. It occurred to me that the children might not even understand that their dad was in that casket. I considered that someday I might regret my decision, but it seemed right at the time.

The navy officers told me that the casket would be sealed in Vietnam and we would not be able to view the body. It was because his body was badly decomposed from being in the murky water and from spending a week in transit back to the states. Larry's commanding officer and the naval chaplain assured me that it was indeed Larry's body in the casket. I decided I had to take their word for it and left it at that.

Helen and I boarded an airplane to Colorado. Helen made arrangements for someone to pick us up at the airport and take us to Yuma. I remember the funeral, but it's as though it happened in slow motion. My parents were there, as well as my sister Geraldine and her husband Ed, my brother Arthur and his wife Fran, and also Larry's sister Elaine. I was so glad to see all of them, but this was not a time of joy. I wished we could have all been together for a different reason.

I had never been to a military funeral before, and it was very special. A United States flag was draped over the casket, which was presented to me after the funeral. When Larry was buried, there was a three-gun salute by the local veterans. Many family and friends attended.

It just did not seem like Larry was in that casket. I wanted so badly to open it and make sure. Was he really gone? Would I never see him again? I had to gather strength and accept this, if I was to move on. I had to be strong for our children. Again I prayed to God for guidance.

After the funeral I telephoned the hospital to check on Michael's condition; I was so worried about him. They told me that Michael was doing much better and was recovering nicely from the double pneumonia. What a relief. *Thank you, God, for once again hearing my prayers*, I thought.

The trip home to Long Beach seemed like it took an eternity. When I finally arrived, I was so happy to see the children and to bring Michael home from the hospital. But this no longer seemed like a home. It was no longer a normal family. We would need to start a new life.

The letters that Larry had said he had sent to each of us were there waiting for me. It was so depressing and yet so special—to think he had written a letter to each child. The letters were only a half page long, but they were, after all, letters their dad had sent to each of them before he died. In the letters he told them he loved them very much and asked them to be good to each other and to me. I would protect those letters forever, so they would have something to call their very own from their father.

The navy kept in touch as promised. The officer in charge of helping me also informed me that we had to move out of naval housing within sixty days because we were no longer eligible for it. I was devastated. It seemed they were adding insult to injury to tell us that so soon after the funeral. *What now?* I wondered. I guess I should have expected it, since there was a long list of families who were waiting to move into the new naval housing.

The navy would pack everything up, move it, and unload it for me at no cost, but it would be a one-time move. The question was where to go! If I went home to Wisconsin I knew I would lean on my parents for help. It was not the thing to do; I was now the head of the household and would have to make a go of it on my own. I knew I had to gather strength for my family by myself before I could settle in Wisconsin. Besides all of Michael's medical records and doctors were there in the Long Beach area. So my choice was made for me; I would stay in Long Beach until I felt it was time to move back to Wisconsin, and the navy could move me then.

Once again, I turned to prayer for strength and guidance; I would straighten up and strengthen up as my mom had taught me, and I would make it. My children were counting on me to be there for them, and I couldn't run and hide. I had to deal with it.

A month had gone by, and I was busy putting things in boxes for our move. I had found a first floor apartment in Long Beach that would be just right for the four of us. Helen was glad I had decided to stay in the area so she could enjoy seeing the grandchildren.

I was still very depressed, and my thoughts kept saying the navy had won the battle. They had had his heart and now they had his body and soul, too. I had only memories. I prayed to God to keep me strong and help me remember the good times we had and not just all the loneliness.

8
Farewell to a Friend

One afternoon about four weeks after the funeral, the lady next door came to visit. She was the one who took care of Diana and Leary while I was in Colorado. She asked me to join her at the Officer's Club for a few drinks that night. Her teenage daughters would babysit. It would be good for me to get out, she said. No, I wasn't ready, especially not anywhere near the base. I would not be good company. *What would I say to anyone who asked where my husband was stationed? How would I respond?* I thought. No, I couldn't deal with the questions. She kept insisting that I would be moved out soon and that she thought a nice quiet evening out with just the two of us would be good not only for me, but for her as well—Farewell to a Friend Night. I said all right, but warned her not to blame me if I wasn't much fun or if I cried.

The Officer's Club was a large, dark room with a bar and a lot of tables set around the floor like a cocktail lounge. There was a dance floor, and soft music was playing. As I recall there were people there, but not many. We ordered our drinks and found a table far enough away from the bar for us to talk privately.

We talked about the navy and how hard it was on the families. I told her that Larry had been planning to retire from the navy and then move to Yuma, Colorado. She spoke about her husband and how she and the girls had moved around a lot and lived overseas with him in another country. It was very relaxing for me, and I was truly enjoying my evening with a friend.

However, the evening didn't end with that quiet conversation. After about an hour three gentlemen approached our table to speak to my neighbor. Apparently they all knew her. Two of the men were in uniform, and one was not. They asked if they could join us. This made me very uncomfortable because I was certain someone was going to ask me where my husband was and I expected to start crying. I wanted to get up and leave, but instead, I froze to the chair.

She introduced all three gentlemen to me, and they sat down. We talked about everything from weather to sports. One of the men asked me to dance. His name was Ken Clark. He was blond, tall, and thin and had a handlebar mustache. I politely refused. He made a joke of it and said he hoped my dog would chew up my Sunday paper just to get even with me for not dancing with him. I laughed and said not only that I didn't have a dog, but that I didn't read the paper, either. They told jokes; we all laughed; and not once did any of them ask about my husband. I don't know if or when she had told them my husband had died, but it seemed strange to me that no one asked where my husband was. That would have been a normal question. I was still wearing my wedding ring so I knew they thought I had one.

When it was time to leave, Ken asked if he could call me and if I would give him my telephone number. I said no, that I had had a nice time, and it was nice meeting everyone, but I had to leave. Two days later my telephone rang, and it was Ken. I asked how he had gotten my telephone number, and he said he had pestered my neighbor, by calling her twice a day, until she gave in and gave it to him. He asked if he could come over, since he knew where I lived. I politely said no. He joked for a while on the telephone and then said he was not giving up that easily and that he would pester me until I gave in.

I was not only annoyed, but also upset. I was furious with my neighbor for giving in to him no matter how much he had pestered her. It was not right. Now I had to deal with it. I wasn't sure, but I gathered from the way he was talking to me that my neighbor had told him about my husband. Again I said thanks, but that I had children to take care of, was in the process of moving, and had no time for relationships.

That evening I thought about his call. I was flattered that he would go to such lengths to find me. He was charming and cute. I pushed the thoughts out of my mind as being ridiculous.

The very next day Ken was knocking on my door. He handed me a newspaper, jokingly explaining that is was a replacement for the one my dog chewed up. But I was packing and the newspaper came in handy. Against my better judgment, I asked him to come in. Ken helped me pack, and he played with the children. He was not in uniform, so I figured maybe he was not in the military. As I recall he wasn't in uniform the night I met him, either. That was OK because I had vowed that I would never again get involved with military life. I was moving out and moving on. There was no place in my life for military men or any men—period. At least not now!

Ken was there every other day offering to help. He also offered to help me move the big stuff. At first I was cautious, but then I was happy to have the extra help because my neighbor and her girls were the only other ones able to help me pack.

Moving a full house by myself with three children in tow seemed an unimaginable feat. I offered to pay Ken for his help, but he would not take any money. He said a fair trade for his help would be my having him over for dinner one night. I told him he had a deal.

About a month later, after I got settled into the apartment in Long Beach, I thought about inviting Ken over to dinner as repayment for his help with the move. What could it hurt? It was just a dinner. Ken was fun, and he made me laugh, which I hadn't been able to do for a long time. Besides, he was good looking, clean, and polite, and he liked the children. I know I hadn't been a widow for very long, and perhaps this was not the right thing to be doing, but Larry was gone now and, after all, we were only having dinner at my house, not going out on a date. I kept trying to convince myself that it was only repayment for his helping me move and that there was no harm in it.

Two weeks later Ken called to ask how things were going and if I was ready for the dinner. Again I thought to myself, "What could it hurt?" So we set a day and time.

I guess I should have known it was wrong because at first I was very nervous and uncomfortable about his being there for dinner. However, Ken was very charming, and we seemed to hit it off right away. My fears melted away. Unfortunately, Helen stopped by the apartment while Ken was there and I could see her disapproval. She took an immediate dislike to him.

The next day Helen and I argued. She felt I was being disrespectful to her son by having a man with us that evening. Perhaps she was right that I shouldn't have had him over, but it was only dinner and only to repay him for helping us. Why was that so wrong? Explaining didn't help; she was very upset with me.

The next week I had an appointment with the naval officer who had helped me with the funeral. He gave me an insurance check for $30,000. Big deal, the money meant nothing to me; it would not bring Larry back. I took the check home put it in my dresser drawer and just tried to forget about it.

The same day a box arrived with all of Larry's personal belongings. It was extremely hard to look at those things. I really did love him, and I missed him. He had been gone so often, I again tried to think of him as just being away, but it wasn't working this time. I sat and cried. It was time for reality; in the box were Larry's wallet, the blue tape player, pictures of us, his dog tags, and various other items.

I was hesitant to listen to the tape in the tape player. Was it the one I had sent him? Was it the one he was recording to send us? Oh how I had hoped it was one he was going to send us, but it was not. It was the last tape the children and I had sent to him. At least I knew he got it and had had a chance to listen to it. He had heard me and the children tell him that we loved him and were anxiously awaiting his return home to us.

The next day, Helen, out of the blue, announced that she had decided it was not Larry in the casket after all so she was going to have the body exhumed. She was going to have the casket opened because, as she said, she needed to be sure it was Larry in there. I argued with her that the navy would not go through all that they did for us if it were not his body in the casket and that she needed to adjust and get on with her life. Of course she was still angry with me for having Ken there the night before so I thought she was saying all those things just to upset me. Believe me, it worked!

Helen hired a lawyer and asked for Larry's casket to be exhumed. I went to see the naval chaplain and explained to him what she was doing. The chaplain assured me again that the body was positively identified as Larry and that we would regret having the casket opened. The chaplain said we would have nightmares from looking at the decomposed body and that there was no point. He assured me that it was up to me and that Helen could not do it if I objected. I asked that he do whatever he had to do to deter Helen so that Larry could rest in peace. The chaplain stated that he would contact Helen and personally go to see her. As much as I wanted to be certain, too, that Larry was in there, I believed the chaplain when he said I would regret it. I wanted to remember Larry the way he was, full of life and laughter, not remembering him as a decomposed mass of flesh and bones. I knew I had to accept his death and move on.

Helen had spoken to the chaplain, but was still not convinced. She was angry with me for not allowing her this closure. I told her I had prayed for guidance and felt I was making the right decision in this matter. We never spoke about it again, although I am sure she never forgave me.

I hadn't seen or heard from Ken in several weeks. I was actually glad because I was feeling ashamed of myself for simply having him over for dinner at my house. I was supposed to be a widow. I was supposed to be in mourning so I was not supposed to be seen in public or with guests. The name widow was new to me and quite frankly I was not totally sure how I was supposed to act, but I was relatively certain it meant that I shouldn't be seen having a good time.

I had a small portable television set, which was our only entertainment, and the picture was going out on it. I knew I had money, I was just afraid to spend it. I had been so used to doing without and making ends meet that I never gave the check a second thought.

Ken called just as I was complaining to the children about the television set. He asked if he could come over to look at it. Perhaps he could fix it for us. He said sometimes it's only a small tube that needs replacing. Reluctantly I agreed. I only hoped Helen wouldn't drop by again.

Ken came over and looked at the television. He said it was not repairable and recommended that I just go buy a new one. *Oh no*, I thought, *I can't do that. I have to save my money.* Ken not only offered to help me pick out a good one, but also he offered to loan me the money to buy it. I was thinking that this was a real gentleman. He really didn't know me and yet he was offering to loan me money to help us out.

After giving it some thought, I decided I could spend some of my money. It was, after all, there for us to get by with. I wasn't going to throw it to the wind, but buying a television couldn't hurt. Larry would have wanted the children to have a TV.

I told Ken I needed to go first to the nearest bank to deposit my insurance check and then we could go shopping. Ken was very diplomatic. He never asked how much the check was for, but must have known it was substantial. Ken offered me some advice. He said the banks were only bonded up to ten thousand dollars each per customer and that I might want to consider dividing and placing my money in different banks. That way if anything happened to one bank, I wouldn't lose all my money. *Now, how nice is that? How thoughtful. I didn't know that.* Of course I wanted the money to be safe. I had no reason to doubt that he was telling me anything but the truth. It never occurred to me to ask the bank, either.

Ken recommended I open a checking account at one of the banks so I would have money readily available when I needed it, for the children of course. It would not have to be a huge sum of money, perhaps five hundred dollars. That sounded good to me. How helpful he was. We went to three different banks, so I am sure he figured out just how much money I had received.

After we took care of the banking, we went to look at television sets. Ken directed me to the stereo department, and we looked at this big beautiful console television that had a radio and record player in it. What a lovely piece of fine furniture it was! I don't remember how much I paid for it, but I was so excited. It was the very first piece of new furniture I had ever bought.

Ken was setting it up for us just as Helen arrived. I was excited and I said to her, "Guess what I just did?"

Helen's reply stunned me.

She said, "You got married."

"What? No," I replied. "I bought a new television set."

Married? Where was that coming from! Surely she wasn't talking about Ken, I barely knew him. I hadn't been dating; I hadn't been out on the town; nor had I even kissed him. I decided that this woman had a problem and that nothing I could say or do was going to fix it. I thought, *Just tolerate her, she is still angry that I wouldn't let her dig up the casket and open it. Maybe someday she will understand and forgive me for my decision.* I explained to her that our television went dead and Ken was kind enough to help us find a new one. She again showed her displeasure with Ken, hugged the children, and left.

I was embarrassed that she treated him like that and tried to explain. Ken said not to worry about it that he understood. What a sweetheart! Would anyone else have been so gracious?

The next few weeks Ken would call or stop by for just a few minutes but never stayed long. My guess was that he did not wish to run into Helen again, and quite frankly, I couldn't blame him.

In the months that followed I had time to think about what I wanted in life and where I wanted to be. I had felt truly content in Hanford, and nothing was stopping me from moving there. *I should go buy a house with the insurance money and just live in peace*, I thought. *After all, my good friends Bob and Marian Taylor are there. It really is a lovely small community and would be a good place for the children, away from the hustle and bustle of big city life.* I had trouble thinking of any reason why I shouldn't move there.

Ken telephoned one night and asked to take me out. This was a real date and he wanted to take me to dinner and then go dancing. *Dancing?* I thought. *Wow, I can't remember the last time I went dancing.* I was lonely, so I said yes that I would go. The evening was wonderful, and Ken swept me off my feet.

We went to an elegant place. The tables had candles, flowers, and tablecloths on them. There was a small dance floor and a person playing piano. At dinner, Ken said that the gentleman always orders for the lady and that he would order for me. He said that I should trust him. I was impressed with his etiquette. Ken introduced me to lobster and showed me how to get it out of the shell. Quite frankly I felt like I had been in a shell. This was all new to me, and it seemed like a dream. Ken was a divine dancer, and we laughed the evening away. I didn't want the evening to end because I felt like Cinderella. Ken was charming, good-looking, and funny, and all the things I never knew or expected to find in a person.

I tried to convince myself that seeing Ken wasn't right because not a whole year had passed since Larry had died, but my reaction to this continued to be, "So what?" He died, I did not. I came up with all the excuses I could to continue seeing Ken. Why not, who was stopping me?

Ken was the complete opposite of Larry. Larry had wanted me to be a stay-at-home wife and mother, but Ken was fun, all laughter and excitement. He made my world spin. I saw the world differently. I heard the music, saw all the beautiful things, and didn't want to let that go. I had no idea that Ken was hiding some deep dark secrets from me. I was feeling like a woman for the first time in a long time, and I let my defenses down far too quickly.

The next major item to fall apart was my car. I had an old Buick with well over 150,000 miles on it. Don't remember what year it was, but I remember it was baby blue. I needed a car. *What am I supposed to do now?* I wondered.

As fate would have it, Ken called almost like he could read my mind. He noticed in my voice that I was not happy. At first he thought it was Helen giving me a hard time. When I explained my problem with the car, he seemed almost relieved. Ken recommended I trade the car in on a new one. "After all," he said, "you can afford it, and the family needs a car." That comment alone should have raised a red flag, but it went right past me. How would he know I could afford it? But he was right. We did need a reliable car.

Talk about nervous, buying a television was one thing, but buying a car was something else. I didn't know anything about cars. Once again, Ken was there to aid the damsel in distress.

He talked me into going into a car showroom and looking at a 1967 Chevy Camaro. He said it was the pace car at the Indy 500. That didn't mean anything to me; I didn't know anything about cars, or the Indy 500, for that matter. This car was brand-new and only had two miles on it. It was yellow and black and was a very sporty-looking car with hideaway headlights.

It was late in the evening, and the salesman did not think Ken was serious about buying this particular car. I know for sure I wasn't thinking of buying this type of car. I had three small children. What did I want with a sports car? I wish I had just left, but I was not even certain where I was.

Ken could see my hesitation and nervousness and asked the car dealer to let us discuss the price in private. I told Ken that he must be joking and that I didn't need a car like that. But Ken kept emphasizing how I was going to get a really good deal on this car. He argued that I could use it as a family car and asked me to think about how proud I would be driving a new car that no one else had ever driven on the road.

The dealer came back and stated that he couldn't let the car go that night anyway because he needed to make sure my credit was good first. Ken told him to check with my bank, that the check was good, and that we would pay cash for the car if he would let us take it that night. He told him that if he did not let us have the car that night, we would walk away and go buy one somewhere else.

The phrase "*we* will pay cash for it" took me by surprise. But I must admit that I was impressed with his no nonsense "take it or leave it" attitude. I never in a million years would have done that on my own. Again, another huge red flag blew right past me!

The salesman spoke with his manager and then told us to take the car. I signed the papers, the dealer handed Ken the keys, and Ken handed them to me. I told him I wasn't driving that car home—especially at night because I didn't know the city that well. He would have to drive. I followed him in his little black Chevy Corvair. All the way home I was asking myself, *What have I done! Am I crazy? I just bought a car off the showroom floor, paid cash for it, and am afraid to drive it.* I realized that was probably what Ken was hoping for because he had no trouble driving it.

If I thought Helen had gone ballistic when I bought the television, I couldn't imagine what she was going to say when she found out that I had bought this car! Oh well, it was too late now; I owned it.

The next day the children and I went for a long ride in our new car. They all seemed comfortable enough, and Diana and Leary really liked it. Michael was not old enough to have an opinion. It was really nice driving a car that had that new-car smell and that I knew would not break down. *Is it so bad that I bought this car?* I thought. I felt better; I felt justified. And Helen would just have to get used to that I was my own person and that she was not in control of what I did or whom I saw.

9

A Big Move and Even Bigger Surprise

I was feeling confident, in both myself and with my beautiful car, to drive with the children to Hanford. I decided to go visit my old friends Bob and Marian and show them I was in charge of my life. While visiting them I mentioned I had thought about buying a house in Hanford. Both Bob and Marian were very happy about that, and just for fun we looked around.

Believe it or not, I found a newly built house on Mulberry Lane that I fell in love with. It was on a corner next to an empty lot with a fenced-in canal beyond that. The back of the house had a big yard and a line of fence, beyond which was a cotton farmer's field. I guess I liked it so much because it seemed private. I liked that there were no immediate neighbor's on either side.

The house was brown and had three bedrooms. One bedroom was done in pink and was perfect for Diana. The other room was light yellow and perfect for the boys. There were two bathrooms. The master bedroom had its own bathroom, and it was done in gold tones. The living room had a fireplace with a mantel. This house was perfect—simply perfect.

After talking with Bob and Marian, I decided I would put some money down on it and would make my getaway from Long Beach and all the associated memories. I had chosen to save the offer from the navy to move me because if I ever wanted to move back to Wisconsin I would use the offer then to save money. I could and I would make this move myself.

It would be hard telling Helen that the children and I were leaving Long Beach, but I was hoping she would see it was for the best—not only for me, but also for the children. After all, it was my life, and I had to make these decisions. It helped that Hanford had good schools and clearly could have positive effects on what kind of future the children and I could have. When I finally did tell Helen, she was disappointed about the children leaving, but was not surprised. I guess not too much of what I did anymore surprised her.

Ken called and said he had been concerned about me because he didn't know where I had gone with the children and we'd been gone for a week. He said he was concerned that I had changed my mind and had headed for Wisconsin. I told him, no, not Wisconsin, but he was correct that I was leaving Long Beach. I told him I had put money down on a house and was moving to Hanford. Ken said jokingly he did not want to live in Hanford. He laughed so I shrugged it off as his usual humor.

Ken said he would help me get moved, so he would know where to find me. Again he laughed so I didn't give the comment a second thought. He arranged for a rental trailer and offered to drive it for me while I drove the car with the children. How nice! I wondered how he could take the time off from work to help me, but I never questioned him. I was glad to have some help. I must admit I felt safer having him travel with us.

Two nights before we were ready to leave for Hanford, Ken asked me to go out again. This time we were going to a place with live music to hear a country band. I got all dressed up to impress him, but he showed up in jeans and cowboy boots. Since I didn't own any jeans or cowboy boots, I stayed dressed the way I was. My black dress coat had a real fur collar on it, and it really looked expensive. In fact, Ken mentioned how elegant I looked in it. He was always complimenting me. His charm sure worked.

We went to this little country bar. It was dark in there, but there was a band playing country music. Apparently Ken knew some of the band members because they called out his name and waved as we came in. I was impressed and loved the music. He introduced me to the bartender and ordered us each a mixed drink. We sat at the bar and listened to the music. Then Ken asked me to dance a slow dance. He was a good dancer and was the perfect gentleman. He surely knew how to sweep me off my feet. When we went back to the bar where we had been sitting, Ken excused himself to go to the men's room. I had a few more sips of my drink.

All of a sudden Ken reappeared, grabbed my arm, and said we were leaving. I asked why because we weren't even done with our drinks yet. Ken said I shouldn't argue with him and pulled my arm harder. I put on my coat, and we went to the car. Ken sped away as fast as he could.

I was starting to feel really dizzy and asked what was going on. Ken said we had been drugged. He said we would need to find a place to park the car to sleep it off. He said it should wear off in about an hour. When he found a place to park, I had no idea where we were. He locked the doors, and, yes, we both passed out. When we came to, I asked him how did he know that we had been drugged and why did he think anyone would do that to us. Ken's only response was that he had started to feel strange and then realized that someone must have dropped something into our drinks while we were dancing and was planning to take all our money. It never occurred to me at the time that I could have been raped or, worse yet, killed.

Instead of being suspicious of his having known that we were drugged and that it would wear off in an hour, I thought he was a hero for saving us. We had been at a place where they knew him by name; it should not have been dangerous. Ken said there was a lesson to be learned there—never walk away from your drink without watching it. Being out on the town was new to me, so I had to believe him. He was so wise. I was very glad we were safe, and I was very grateful to Ken. I thought about my children and what would have happened to them if something had happened to me. Oh God, what a horrible thought.

When we got to Hanford a couple of days later, Ken was very impressed with my choice of houses. He asked what I had paid for it and how much I had put down on it. I guess it didn't matter to me if he knew; we were becoming very close, so I told him. I also said I was planning to use the money I had left to get it professionally decorated and then was going to pay the house off so I didn't have to worry about any more payments. Ken told me it was foolish to pay a house off because if you ever decided to sell it you will never get the full equity out of it. And the interest from a mortgage could be used as a tax deduction. I figured he was right because I didn't know anything about mortgages or tax breaks. I had never owned any property before. How smart he was. *Good looking and smart, too*, I thought. I felt he had done nothing but help me so far, and I was beginning to lean on him a lot. Ken said he would hitch a ride back to Long Beach, and he left.

Marian and Bob did not like Ken. They were concerned that he was a phony, a con man trying to take me for the money I had left. I assured them he was not like that and they had to be wrong.

Several months went by with no word from Ken. One night I received a telephone call from a man who identified himself as Ken's younger brother Johnny. He said Ken needed to see me and asked if I would come to San Diego to see him. I could not get any specifics from him and was concerned that Ken had been hurt. Johnny assured me Ken was all right, but it was very important that I see him. I asked Bob and Marian to watch the children, and I made arrangements to go to San Diego.

Johnny met me at the airport and took me to Ken's parents' home where I met his mom and dad, Reba and John. They told me that Ken was in the United States Navy brig, in other words, jail. I suddenly realized that Ken was in the navy and was probably AWOL—absent without leave—all the times he had been with me. *How could he do that to me knowing full well I want nothing to do with any military servicemen?* I thought. I was angry and upset. I had trusted him! I wanted to go back to the airport and get out of there.

Johnny and his parents asked that I at least see Ken and hear his story. They were very sweet and thoughtful people. I figured that since they were really nice people Ken couldn't be that bad. I felt I at least owed it to him to hear what he had to say. *I'm already here, so I might as well see him*, I thought.

The next day Johnny took me to the San Diego Naval Base where I visited with Ken. Johnny left us alone to talk. Ken told me he wanted me to know the whole truth because I had been good to him, he really cared about me, and he hoped we could maybe have a future together.

The story he told me knocked my socks off. Ken said that he was married with a son, also named Ken, who was the same age as my Leary. Ken also said that he was in the navy and his term was almost up. His job was a deep-sea diver. He said he did welding and repairs to the ships under water. He said there were nights when he would go home to his wife and notice that some of his clothes had been worn and his shoes were scuffed. He said he figured his wife Juanita was fooling around on him, so he came home early one day to try to find out what was going on. He found his wife in their bed with another man. Ken said he was so hurt that he got a knife from the kitchen and told the guy he was going to kill him. Ken said both his wife and the guy ran off, called the police, and reported the incident as an attempted murder. He swore to me that he never cut them; he merely wanted to scare them. He got scared when he heard there was an attempted murder charge out on him, and he fled to Long Beach where he had been living for over a month when he met my neighbor at the Officer's Club. I asked how he could have the nerve to go into an Officer's Club when he was not only AWOL but also wanted for attempted murder. He said he was like a hunted fox, hiding right under their noses, and it became a game of hide and seek. Ken continued to say that after he met me he decided he was going to have to turn himself in if he was going to have any life at all, especially with me. He said the attempted murder charges were dropped, and he was now just serving his time for being AWOL. His wife, Juanita, had fled from San Diego and took everything with her, including his son. He had no idea where they were. When he turned himself in, he begged his brother Johnny to contact me so he could tell me the truth.

I sat there in disbelief. I really wanted him to laugh and say he was just joking, but that did not happen. Ken explained that he only had a few months left to go in the navy and would not re-enlist because he did not like navy life, either. He told me that he did enjoy being a deep-sea diver and that he was a certified underwater welder, too. However, he didn't think there were jobs outside of the military like that and he would have to find some other type of work.

Ken said the reason he didn't tell me the truth from the beginning was that he knew that if I knew I would want nothing to do with him. Actually he was right on that one. He pleaded with me to give him a chance at a real life. He said he felt so good being with me and the kids—he felt like a new person. He promised me he would never hurt me or the children in any way. I told Ken I could neither answer him, nor promise him anything. I had to think about my children and my new house. I couldn't live the navy life again, and he knew that. Lord knows I said it often enough. Before I left he asked me to at least consider writing to him. I told him I would think about it.

I went back to Hanford and told no one about my conversation with Ken. *What would Helen, Bob, and Marian think of me for even writing to a guy like this? Could they be right about him? Am I falling under the spell of this blond-haired jailbird? Is he a con man?* I wondered.

I figured he had to be telling the truth about them dropping the attempted murder charges; otherwise, he would be in regular jail not just the brig. I had to give him credit for turning himself in. I really liked him, but this was just such a shock. *Would I be able to continue seeing him knowing this secret about him? Would my family be safe with him? I have to think about the children. I have to be cautious.* I thought many times about how much he had already done for me, including saving me from the drug dose that night. If he wanted to hurt me, I had given him every opportunity and he hadn't done that. I didn't like the secret, but I was truly smitten with this man. I shouldn't even have given him a second thought; I should have said no to this relationship.

The very next week my children got a letter from Ken—not me, my children. He asked them to please convince their mother to write to him and told them that he really cared about them and truly missed their mother. It was funny the way he worded it, and I had to laugh. What a very clever person he was—especially trying to get to me through the children. The children thought it was funny, too. I did write to him even though my better judgment said not to. I was hooked!

Several weeks later he was out of the brig and back to deep-sea diving. Whenever he would get a three-day weekend, he would come to Hanford. The man just swept me off my feet. He was so much fun. He was changing my life from drab and dreary, filling it with fun, laughter, and excitement.

As time went by, Ken begged me to come to San Diego with the children for a few weeks until he was out of the navy. After all, it was only a few weeks. He would get an apartment for all of us, and when he was discharged, we would immediately depart back to Hanford. Neither one of us liked the long distance between us!

I was apprehensive but gave in. *San Diego here we come*, I thought. Bob and Marian told me I was making a huge mistake, but I really liked Ken and wished they had liked him, too.

I only packed what I thought we would need for a few weeks, and away we went. Navy life with Ken was not the same as it was with Larry because Ken was home every night like men with normal jobs. He did not have to go out to sea for weeks or months on end.

The apartment was on the first floor and in a nice neighborhood. It had two bedrooms, a small living room, and a little kitchen. It was only temporary and would be just fine.

One day to the children's delight, Ken brought home a live baby octopus in a pail of water for the children to see. All the neighborhood children came to see it, too. My children were now popular in the neighborhood, and they seemed happy.

We had lobster sandwiches because Ken would bring home lobster almost every night. He brought home seashells, abalone shells, clamshells, and once a giant clamshell. It was huge and beautiful. It was a gift for me, and I knew exactly where I would put it when I got back to Hanford.

He had a plan to make a mailbox from a diver's deep-sea helmet. What a neat idea! The mailman would open the faceplate to put the mail in. How unique!

This man mesmerized me. He could make me feel like no one else ever had. I was totally under his spell.

Ken came home one night and said he had found a good deal on a foreign car. A small, black MG! He said the guy would take the big clamshell he had given me and a few hundred dollars cash for the car. Ken said he would get me another clamshell and asked if I would loan him the money so he could buy it. I don't remember how much money it was exactly, but it didn't seem like a lot at the time, so I gave it to him. Ken bought the car and called it Mr. Toad. Ken loved that car. It was his pride and joy. I must admit I was not really thrilled with giving up the giant clamshell, but Ken reminded me he could get me another one before we left San Diego.

Ken was very much into possessions and favors for other people. He always wanted to make other people happy by giving them things. One night Ken told me his most ultimate wish and dream was to buy his brother Johnny an Austin Healy sports car—not a new one, a used one. It was something his brother had longed for all his life, and Ken wanted to be able to give it to him.

I truly hate to admit this, but we went shopping. We found a used Austin Healy and gave it to Johnny as a gift with the stipulation that if he ever decided to get rid of it he would return it to Ken. Johnny was beaming, and Ken was so happy to be able to make his brother's dream come true. I guess seeing them happy made me happy, too, although it was my money that we had spent.

The giving did not stop there. His parents decided they were going to buy a house about five miles from the Tijuana border. They did not have the down payment and asked if I would loan them the money. They would give it back as soon as they closed the deal on the other house.

I felt proud to help his parents because they had truly been good to me. They had threatened Ken on my account. They said that if he ever hurt me or the children, they would disown him. Ken did not take it well that they had threatened to disown him, but he said that he wasn't planning to ever let us go. He said he would always be good to us because we had given him a second chance at life.

His parents did pay the money back as promised. Their new house was beautiful. The smell of a new house with new carpeting throughout was nice. I questioned their choice of furniture, though, since the dining room had red velvet chairs that I was petrified the children would spill something on. We didn't go there very often for that very reason.

Ken said he loved me and asked me to marry him. I turned him down. I said I loved him, too, but I would lose my benefits from the government if I remarried. With him getting out of the navy soon, what would we live on in Hanford? Besides, as far as we knew, he was still married. Ken assured me Juanita must have gotten a divorce by now. I just said no, not until we know where our future is headed. Ken stated that he loved me and the children and wanted us to get married. He even said that he wanted to adopt the children.

I told Ken about the promise I had made to Larry and explained that nothing he could ever say would convince me to break that promise. I was sorry, but I just could not do that. Ken became furious and said I had to stop living in the past and get on with my life. I told him I was ready to move on with my life, but a promise was a promise, and I could not and would not break it. If he loved me he should respect my wish to keep that promise. End of discussion! I was proud of myself for standing up to him and for honoring Larry's memory.

While we were still in San Diego, Ken broke his leg. I don't remember how, but it was his right leg. He had a cast all the way up to his knee, so he was home every day for a while. Ken couldn't deep-sea dive with a cast on his leg, so they gave him medical leave.

One day I received a telephone call from the school. The teacher wanted me to know what Leary had said to the class. The teacher asked the children to stand up, one at a time, and tell what their fathers did for a living. When it was Leary's turn, he told the class that his dad just sat in his big yellow chair and yelled at his wife and kids to go get him a beer. I was embarrassed, but Ken thought it was funny. I explained to the teacher that Ken was a deep-sea diver, but that he had broken his leg and couldn't work right now. She understood and laughed with us.

Ken's broken leg did not stop him from driving. He couldn't drive the MG because it was too tight with the cast on, so he drove the Camaro. He would prop his leg over the console and would use his left foot for the gas and brake pedal. I was very nervous about this, but there was no convincing Ken it was unsafe.

One day he was in the Camaro driving by himself and eating a taco when the car in front of him began continually hitting the brakes. Ken said he was watching that car and since it never really stopped, he assumed that the driver just kept touching the brakes by accident. He said that all of a sudden the car ahead of him was at a complete stop and it was too late; Ken ran into the back of it. He was not hurt, and the driver of the other car was not hurt. The car Ken hit from behind only had one taillight broken. We thought my Camaro was totaled because the hideaway headlights were pushed so far under the hood they were almost in his lap. My 1967 Chevy Camaro was mangled. I was crushed. I loved that car.

Thank the Lord that I had full coverage on it and the insurance would take care of it. Wrong! They insisted the car could be fixed. We had to get estimates and get it repaired. The car did not seem as trustworthy any more after that, and I was almost afraid to drive it. It just wasn't right.

Ken and I went car shopping again. We traded the Camaro in on an Oldsmobile Vista Cruiser. I don't remember what year it was, but it was relatively new and had a skylight. It was a big, family car. I was happy with it.

The next month, Ken's cast came off, and he went back to work. Everything seemed fine, and he would be home every night. One night he came home driving a Jeep. I asked where the MG went, and he said he had traded the MG even up for the Jeep. I couldn't believe it; he loved that MG. Ken said that where we were going we would need a more stable vehicle and a Jeep was just what we needed. Whatever, at least he didn't ask for money this time.

Ken's birthday was coming up, February 7. I wanted to do something very special for him, so I surprised him with a gold ring that had three diamonds in it.

It cost me almost five hundred dollars. He was really happy with it, like I said once before, material things meant everything to him, and he had never had a diamond before.

I knew we would soon be leaving for Hanford, but was not ready for what was about to happen. I had no clue the time was as close as it was.

Ken came home around 5:00 PM and said we were leaving that night. I said, "No, we aren't ready to go yet. What about all the packing?" He said we had just five hours to pack up what we could because the rest was going to be left behind; we were leaving no later than 10:00 PM. He sent the children to their bedroom to pick up their toys and pack them or they would be left behind; he told them he did not care if all their toys were left behind. Ken said he had some last-minute paperwork with the navy to clean up and left.

This was not the same man who had been so warm and caring. This man was demanding and strict. How could I manage this? He wasn't even helping. I went into panic mode and was running around trying to pack as much as I could. The children didn't totally comprehend what was happening; they just wanted to play with their toys, not pack them. What a mess it was, with toys everywhere, but I couldn't help them. I had too many other things to do myself.

Ken returned around 8:00 PM and started throwing cartons and things in the U-Haul truck he had brought home. He again warned the children that if they didn't pick up the toys they would be left behind. I tried to get them to pack their toys, but they were tired; after all, it was their bedtime.

Ken was not joking. At precisely 10:00 PM the vehicles were as loaded as they were going to get and he was ready to pull out. The jeep would stay behind and he would come back for it in a few days. I still did not have everything packed and the children's toys were still all over the bedroom. He refused to wait and said to leave them. "Whatever is left stays here!" he yelled. He said he had warned the children if they did not pick up and pack their toys, the toys would stay behind. I said, "No, my mom made those doll clothes for Diana, and I am not leaving them." He was angry with me and said the landlord could donate them to a charity because he meant what he said. It was the children's fault for not doing as they were told, not ours. I was very upset with him about this and tried again to make him wait so I could clean it up. He said, "You don't have a choice. We are leaving. Go get in the car!"

I did as I was told and cried for the first few miles out of San Diego. *How can he be so cruel? Some of those doll clothes are so delicate, and they are so special—little sweaters my mom knitted and little dresses she made for Diana's dolls. There are other toys, too, that should have been packed; it wasn't just Diana's toys. We left things they got for Christmas, things they will surely miss, and things they could have cherished forever*, I thought.

I was not only angry with him, but I was angry with myself for not standing up to him. *Is this a sign of things to come? Have I become his slave to obey his every request? Lord, I hope not. Where is the sweet protector that I fell in love with! This man is not someone I want to spend my life with nor have my children around. He is mean and demanding, even abusive*, I thought.

10
Abuse

It was around 2:00 AM when we arrived in Hanford, and I was truly glad to be back in my new house. We were all so tired we just went to bed and left everything in the vehicles until the next morning. That was OK with me because I wasn't speaking to him anyway.

The next day Ken was as sweet as could be and apologized for being so sharp. He was hugging me, kissing me, and asking me to understand that he just wanted to get it done. I told him I understood that part, but that I was upset about leaving behind the things my mom made that were important to me. Then he told me some of it was my fault, though, because I didn't make the children do as they were told. If they had done as they were told everything would be here with us.

Ken liked to play mind games and always seemed to know how to get me to think his way. He would turn something around to make it my fault, and he was so convincing that by the time he was done I was convinced he was right. That alone should have been a wake up call for me, a huge red flag again, but it was not.

We had many happy days, too. I truly loved Ken and wanted the relationship to work. I had to make it work. He always told me that if the man of the house is happy the rest of the family will be happy, too. I believed that because when he was happy we could all relax and enjoy what we had. After all, we had a new house, new furniture, and a nice car. What more could we ask for!

The answer to that was a horse—a horse for Ken! He convinced me it would be good for the children to learn about animals and how to take care of them. He wanted me to picture what fun they would have riding, with his help, of course. He bought a white albino, and we rented a pasture behind our house about two blocks away.

I am not sure what breed the horse was. All I remember was that its eyes were almost blue and the horse was truly white. This horse didn't last long because it would throw Ken off when he tried to get him to cross a creek or ditch. From what Ken could figure, the horse was either blind or nearly blind.

Ken decided to sell the horse to a man who wanted a horse for his little girl. I objected because I believed the horse was dangerous. I told Ken I thought he had said the horse was almost blind. Ken would respond to that with comments such as no, he just doesn't look too good. He was trying to use humor to cover up the fact that he was selling a blind horse to a man who wanted it for his little girl. I asked Ken if he had no conscience, and he said he wouldn't be able to sell the horse if he told the truth. I wonder to this day if that little girl ever got hurt. I pray she did not. The thought of a child getting hurt because of Ken's selfishness and deception made me sick. But nothing I said could stop him.

Of course, when he sold that horse, he bought two more—a huge gelding and a pinto. The gelding was dark red, so he named it Red. The pinto was black-and-white, and I named it Apache. Red did not like me for some reason, even though I made every attempt to be his friend. I would go to the field during the day and brush him just to get the horse to know me better. But when I would attempt to ride him, he would throw me off every time.

I fell really hard one time and was not going to get back on, but Ken forced me. He said if I didn't get back on I may be afraid to ever ride again. I did as I was told and cut the ride really short. After that I just stopped riding Red and worked with Apache instead. It wasn't until years later when arthritis set in that I found out I had broken my collarbone during my fall.

Apache was a gentle horse, and I could ride him bareback. Apache did not like Ken and would run from him every time he got near. One day Ken decided he was not going to let this horse get away anymore. Ken caught up to him with a rope. Apache reared up, knocked Ken to the ground, and stomped on him. Ken was so angry I thought he was going to shoot my horse. In fact, he made that threat but didn't follow through with it. I should have learned from the sense my horse had of Ken, but I did not.

The children really liked the horses. Ken would run Red until he was tired, and then he would put all three children on the saddle and lead the horse around the field to cool it down. They were always excited about going to see the horses. Some days we would make a picnic basket and spend the day under a shade tree in the field with the horses. It was really a nice family outing.

By now the money was getting thin. I had not paid off the house as I had first intended to do, mainly because of Ken's advice. I still had fifteen thousand dollars set aside for the children. It was in a bank in Long Beach. I thought I should save that much for them. They would each get five thousand dollars when they were adults. I got half, and they got half. I felt by then the interest alone would give each of them a nice start for their futures. I figured if Ken didn't know it was there, it was safe. I would just have to make do with what we had, the monthly allotment from the government.

Ken finally got a job. Hanford did not have any deep-sea diving jobs, so he became a bartender in a dinner house. He was gone most nights, and the children and I would have pleasant evenings together.

Michael was doing really well as far as his health was concerned, but I was having trouble potty training him. I worked with him, but I guess he just wasn't ready. There were times when Ken would get so angry at Michael for wetting himself that he would take Michael outside and turn the hose on him. I would scold Ken for scaring Michael, and Ken would defend himself by saying Michael only wets because he is too lazy to come in to go to the bathroom and that he has to learn. I told Ken that turning a hose on him was not going to help; it would just make it worse. Ken said, "Fine, then you deal with it."

I tried again to get Michael potty trained, but once again, he wet himself in front of Ken. I wondered if he wasn't doing it on purpose just to aggravate Ken but quickly dismissed the thought. Why would any child do that if he knew he would be punished? This time, Ken decided to put a dress on Michael to embarrass him. I didn't like it, but at least he wasn't physically hurting him. Michael didn't seem to mind the dress, and that made Ken even angrier. Ken picked Michael up by the dress and shoved him up against the wall. I stepped in, pushed Ken away, and pulled Michael away from him. I was still afraid of Michael's heart and did not want anything to happen to him. I told Ken that Michael was just a little boy who had had open-heart surgery. "Just leave him alone," I said. Ken scolded me and said if I kept interfering with his discipline, we would never get him trained and the children would not do as they were told, either. If we were going to have good children, we would have to work together. I agreed with him on that in principle, but thought to myself, *not if he is going to abuse them*. I was grateful when, soon after that, Michael was trained. Another crisis was over with!

Most of the time, Ken was a happy-go-lucky, party person. We would have people over all the time. When Ken was happy, we all were happy.

One summer, Ken decided we should have a swimming pool in our backyard. He thought we should buy the lot next to us so we would have the whole corner. He had it all landscaped in his mind. I told Ken I didn't know how to swim and neither did the children. Of course he didn't want to hear that, after all, he was a deep-sea diver, and he assured me he would teach all of us. I didn't like the sound of that. He designed the pool and had a builder come to the house and give us an idea of how long it would take to put it in. I thought to myself, *a swimming pool would be nice because it gets so hot in the summer here*. Sometimes, it got up to 105 degrees. I knew the children would love it.

But where was all this money going to come from! I told Ken we couldn't afford it, that we were living from payday to payday. He said, nonsense, take it out of your bank in Long Beach. Oh my God, he had found the bankbook. I explained that the money in that account belonged to the children. I had spent all the other insurance money on various things. I reminded him about all the vehicles I had bought since I met him. Ken got angry with me. He said the money was given to me and it belonged to me, not the children. And, after all, wouldn't they benefit from the swimming pool? There went the mind games again. He worked on me until I gave in. We bought the lot adjacent to our house and had the swimming pool installed as he had designed it.

I must admit there were times when he actually scared me with his thinking and I wondered how I could get myself out of the relationship. *Do I really want to continue down this path*? I asked myself. I prayed for help to just maintain, to keep my children out of harms way, and to let us be happy with all the good things we had. I loved Ken, yet there was always a voice in the back of my mind that said be cautious.

At one point, Ken wanted me to buy a tavern on the other side of town. I wanted no part of it because that type of work would require us to be there all the time. We had a family, and I couldn't run that kind of business. Besides if we couldn't find someone we trusted to work for us, we could loose everything and we would have no time off. No, this was not something I wanted to do! No charm of any kind was going to convince me that it would be a good business decision. I wish I had kicked his behind to the curb on day one and saved all of us the aggravation.

11

Abuse and Meanness

I loved this man so much, yet when he got angry, he was mean and powerful. Just as I was seriously thinking about how to end the relationship, I found out I was pregnant. *Oh my God, what am I going to do* now? I wondered. I told Ken I was pregnant, and, without blinking an eye, he told me to get an abortion. I said no I wouldn't do that and flatly refused; an abortion was not an option. When he realized I would not be swayed on this matter, he dropped the request. He even tried to make it seem like he was happy for us.

The next situation with the children came when Michael tried to flush his wooden blocks down the toilet. Michael had seen that the little plastic animals went down, so he wondered why the wooden blocks didn't. I understand children's reasoning of that kind, but Ken was not amused. He took the toilet apart to get the block out and then put the toilet back together again, only to find out another block was still stuck in there. Ken was so furious his face turned beet red. I knew instantly Michael was in trouble again. When Ken had the toilet back together he asked me to bring Michael in there. I figured he would show him what he had had to do to get the block out and explain to Michael not to throw blocks in the toilet. But to my horror he quickly picked Michael up, turned him upside down, stuck his head in the toilet, and flushed it. I pounded on Ken to let him go and pulled Michael away from him. Ken just walked out of the house, and I didn't see him until late that evening. Quite frankly, pregnant or not, at that point I wouldn't have cared if he had never come back. That was a clear sign of abuse.

But once again, Ken came home apologetic. He said he had lost his temper, he was truly sorry, and it would never happen again. He explained that he was all right until he had to take it all apart for the second time, and then he lost his cool. He was using mind games again. He knew just what he had to do to get to me. Ken actually got on his knees to plead and beg for forgiveness. It was Michael he should apologize to, not me. The poor boy was almost traumatized by a fear of being flushed down the toilet. I was crying because all I wanted was for us to be a happy family. Ken promised to make it up to Michael, and, as usual, I believed him.

I know at the time I was sick to my stomach with his meanness, but writing this down now makes me even sicker. Why did I ever allow him to have this type of control over me? It was without a doubt child abuse. It was all about control, and it seemed he had it all.

Diana did not go without problems either. One day we had a knock on our door, and it was a social worker. Diana did not want to wear her coat for recess at school so she told the teacher she didn't have a coat. The social worker was checking our house to see if we needed welfare aid or help in any way. I told the gentleman that Diana had a better coat than he was wearing and that it was probably in her locker. He said that he could see we had a nice house and that he was sorry to bother us, but he asked us to understand that they had to check it out in case there was need or child neglect. Needless to say, Diana met with Ken's wrath. He did not see any humor in having a social worker come to our house. But as I recall he just screamed at Diana and told her if she didn't wear her coat at school she would get a good spanking. There didn't seem to be a problem after that.

As for Leary, Ken would compare him to what he imagined his son, little Ken, would be like now, because they were, after all, the same age. Ken expected much from Leary, and when Ken said jump he expected Leary to jump and not ask why.

I asked Ken why he was so strict and why he expected so much from the children. Ken told me that he was in court once for child abuse. He said his son, little Ken, would repeatedly run into the street to play and would never look for traffic. Ken said he tried to explain to the child that he might get hurt, but little Ken didn't listen. One time he watched as a car almost hit his son. Ken said it was then he realized he needed to get little Ken's full attention once and for all, so he whipped him with a belt, which left bruises. Ken said he didn't hit him that hard and that the child didn't have any broken bones or anything. Besides, he claimed, kids bruise easily. He asked the judge to put himself in his place and consider whether he would rather do whatever was necessary to get the child's attention or just let him run into the street and watch him die. He told the judge if he was not allowed to discipline the child after repeatedly trying to talk to him that he would sue the judge if his son died from running into the street. Ken said the judge dismissed the case. That was Ken's version of the story so I am not sure if it was true or not. As I have said many times, he played mind games.

There were other times when I questioned why Ken was so strict with the children. After all, they were just children. He would often admit that he was strict, but argue that they behaved well because of it and that we could be proud of them. He asked me to consider how many times we had been complimented on how well behaved the children were. Our family could go to a restaurant and be proud. We could eat more quietly with a family of five than most people could! Ken was playing the mind games again. He wanted me to believe he was strict because he loved them and wanted to be proud of them. He did not consider his treatment of the children abusive.

Ken told me about his childhood, and it was not a pleasant one. His mom had polio, and the children, Gene, William, Ken, and Johnny were sent to live with relatives. Ken said he lived with a religious family and was required to dress up and pray for almost an hour before the evening meal. After the meal the children were sent right to bed upstairs and not allowed to come downstairs for any reason, not even to use the bathroom. And they had to be quiet all evening. He said many nights he quietly opened the window and urinated through it because he didn't know what else to do. If he went downstairs, he got whipped with a belt. Ken said he just learned to stay upstairs no matter what. That would explain, not excuse, some of the strictness he was trying to instill in the children.

Ken would often say how lucky we were to have three angels. I was proud of them, but it never registered that they were well behaved because they were living in fear. I don't recall one time that any of them came to me and said they were afraid of Ken. Maybe it was because they thought I would confront him and they would get into trouble again. I loved my children deeply. I wanted them to be good, but I wanted them to be happy, too. I think back to the abuse they were subjected to and am so ashamed I allowed them to live like that. I hope they can forgive me for not throwing him out and instead following my own selfish need for companionship.

Ken knew I would never take any physical abuse from him, which I'm sure is why he got so good at the mind games. It was still abuse, mental abuse, but I did not recognize that. He would scream at me in anger, but he never raised a hand to me, except for one time.

I went to the kitchen to take a couple of Tylenol because I had a headache. Ken, still arguing, followed me into the kitchen. It was not uncommon for me, like many people, to dump a bunch of pills out of a bottle, take the one or two I want, and then pour the rest back in. So this time when I took the bottle and a whole bunch fell out into my hand, Ken yelled at me, "You aren't taking all those pills!" Just for spite, I quickly threw them all in my mouth, and he lunged at me ripping my mouth open to spit the pills out. I wouldn't so he punched me in the chest so hard that I had no choice but to spit them out. Then he hugged me and said that I should never do that again, it scared him, he loved me, and he did not want to lose me.

The next day, my ribs were really hurting, so I went to the doctor. They took X-rays and found that I had two broken ribs. The doctor wanted me to file charges against Ken for physical abuse, but I refused, saying it was an accident. Ken never would have done that to me had I not put all those pills in my mouth. It had only happened one time and I thought he deserved a second chance. The doctor asked if I was trying to commit suicide, and I said absolutely not, I had my children to worry about. The doctor dismissed the event as an accident. That was the only time Ken ever attacked me physically. His abuse to me was mental and emotional with his constant mind games. But at the time, I did not realize it was still abuse of another form.

Knowing that I was pregnant, Ken tried again to convince me to marry him. Again I said no. He was not an easy man to deal with when he was angry. I sent the children outside because I did not want them to hear us arguing. I did not want to lose him, but even though I was pregnant, I just wasn't sure getting married was what I should do. I still hadn't seen any paperwork that proved he was divorced. Would we be legally married or would it be bigamy? He kept saying I didn't trust him and that he was hurt that I didn't believe he loved me. But I had never said that. I believed he loved me. I just wasn't certain that getting married was the answer. I had made a decision when I was eighteen that may not have been right for me, and I didn't want to do that again.

We argued again about my living in the past. He said it irritated him that I still had letters that Larry had written to me. He wanted to know why I was hanging on to them if I was ready to move on. He asked me to burn the letters to prove to him once and for all that I could let go of the past. To keep the peace, I reluctantly agreed, but only if he would do me one favor, give me the space to do it myself. He said fine, if that was what needed to happen. Ken started the fireplace so I had a fire. I went to the closet and got the box that contained all the letters. I sat on the floor by the fireplace, opened the box, took one letter out, and started to read it. This immediately infuriated Ken, and he grabbed the letter and the box out of my hands and emptied the box in the fire. I tried to grab some of them back from the fire, but he pushed me away. He held me back so I couldn't remove anything from the flames. I stood there in disbelief watching everything go up in flames. I cried and screamed at him that he had no right to do that. The children's letters were in there, the telegram, and the last tape for the children from their father. The last thing they would ever get from him—a memory I could never ever replace. I was actually sick and felt like I was going to vomit. Ken tried to comfort me by saying the past was gone, that I had proven to him that I loved him, and that it was time to move on. He said he had done it for me, to prevent me from reliving the past and pain of reading each letter. *Yea right, for me! He has done this for me?* I thought. I felt hatred for him at that moment. He had no compassion, no understanding of my pain. I tried to explain about the last letter to the children and the last tape. Ken said that their father was dead and that saving that stuff would have just caused them more pain.

What will I tell the children when they grow up? How can I ever tell them I let Ken convince me to burn my letters and in the process I burned their father's last words to them—something they would have cherished? How could I allow him to control me like that? My children would never understand that kind of control. I prayed to God that my children would forgive me some day. This secret has pained me forever, and I will never forgive myself.

As soon as Ken left the house, I hid the rest of the things I had saved. No more burning—he would never find the rest of the things I had. I had to hide Larry's letter sweater from high school, metals from the navy, pictures, albums, flag, and uniform of dress blues and whites. I had to hide them really well and decided to place them in the kitchen, far back in a cabinet where he would never look. He was not going to make me destroy anymore. He burned part of my heart that day, and it left deep, deep scars. How could I hate someone so much and yet love him, despise him and yet not want him to leave? I was torn between my past and my future. I knew I would survive, yet I wondered where my life was going. I felt so hollow inside, so empty.

When Ken returned the mind games began as soon as he came through the door. He came home with flowers and was profusely apologetic for not allowing me to deal with the letters. He said it was his own selfish jealousy that made him react like that. He said he felt insecure since he had asked me twice now to marry him and I had turned him down both times. He claimed that I had to forgive him because he couldn't live without me and the children. I fell for his sob story once again and told him I understood why he had done it. What I did not say was that I was never, ever going to forgive him for it. I guess I wasn't a strong enough person to tell him outright that I hated him for doing that to me. I should have been honest and told him how I felt, but I did not.

As time went by, Ken talked more and more about his own son. He talked about looking for him and kidnapping him. Ken said he figured Juanita would have returned to her hometown, and he would find out what school little Ken was attending and he would just go and snatch him. I was horrified that he would even think of doing this to a child. I told Ken his son would be more than welcome in our family, but he would have to do it legally or not at all. The subject was soon dropped. I believed the clincher was "legally." It had not occurred to me at the time, but Ken was still afraid of the legal system and what I might find out about him. I often wondered if he was hiding something else from me. But since he dropped the subject, so did I, and I removed it from my thoughts.

12
Practical Joker

It was about this time that Ken traded the Jeep. He traded it for a family room bar and a .308 rifle. I could not understand why he made such a foolish trade, but months later I learned that he had lost a bet and had to make the trade. The bar was a beautiful piece of furniture made out of monkeypod wood. At least that's what he told me. It had an unusual type of grain in it. And, for all I knew, it came from the Orient like he said. We had no place for this bar, so it sat in our garage. But with all the entertaining we did, I was certain he would make use of it. The rifle took shells like I had never seen before, with really long points.

Ken decided we were going deer hunting at Patterson Mountain that year. When Ken said we, he meant just the two of us. He said it was a surprise getaway for me, and he arranged for our neighbor Cindy to come to stay with the children for two days and nights. I had never been hunting but had total respect for guns and chose never to handle any.

Patterson Mountain was north of Fresno, and the countryside was breathtaking. We camped in a tent that Ken had borrowed and hunted the next day before making the trip back home. The camping was kind of fun because I had never done it before and found the air in the woods to be refreshing. The air was cool, but we were not really cold until we saw that the water for our morning coffee had frozen overnight. It was then we realized just how cold the mountains were. Ken made breakfast over a wood fire and cleaned all the cooking utensils. Actually I was feeling kind of special that he was doing this for me. Silly me, I actually believed he was doing this for me. When he was done, everything was packed up and put in the car. Then we went hunting.

I was not much of an outdoors type of person, and Ken complained that I was making too much noise walking through the woods. Quite frankly I did not know you could walk quietly through thick brush and did the best I could under the circumstances. It was hard enough trying to keep up with him. I had never hunted before and wasn't even sure what we would find. It was getting to be mid afternoon, and I was tired from walking through the woods all day.

All of a sudden Ken motioned for me to stop. He saw a buck and took two shots at it. My ears rang from the sound of the gun, but I was excited for Ken. He thought he shot the buck because he didn't see it run off. We went down one side and up the other of a steep embankment, and sure enough there was this big, beautiful buck. If I remember correctly, it was a twelve-point buck. Ken gutted out the deer, and we tried to pull him through the thicket. If we managed to pull it ten feet, we were lucky. It was so heavy. It was getting to be dusk, and there was no way we were going to get this buck to our car before dark. Ken said there was no way he was leaving this trophy behind, so he cut the head off the body. He gave the rifle to me to carry, and he carried the deer head. I was certain that leaving that body behind was illegal or something, but Ken assured me the wild animals would eat the deer meat so I shouldn't worry about it. We followed the trail, and it was getting darker and darker. The deer head was heavy, even for Ken, and he carried it on his back and shoulders while hanging on to the rack of horns. I told Ken I thought it was dangerous to carry it that way because someone might shoot him thinking he was the buck. Ken said something like if I was so smart then I should carry it. I was not about to carry that head, so I kept quiet and continued walking. When we got to the car, he put the head in the back of the station wagon and covered it up with a blanket so it looked like the body was still attached. I asked why he did that, and he replied that if someone stopped us it would look like we had the whole deer.

As Ken was driving down the mountainous rode, he handed me the rifle and told me to unload it. I said no, I wasn't touching it; he should stop and unload it. Ken was furious and said we needed to get down from the mountain or we could get a fine for coming out after dark with a buck. Ken told me how to pump the rifle and said he would count the shells because he knew how many were in there. I did as I was told against my better judgment. Ken counted and said now the rifle should be empty. He wanted me to point it to the floor and pull the trigger. I shouted, "Are you crazy? We are on a mountainside. You could blow out a tire and kill us. We have children at home who need us. I won't do it." Ken kept driving and grabbed the rifle from my hands. He snarled at me to put down my window. I rolled down the window, and he aimed the gun, across my face, out the window and pulled the trigger. The rifle went off, spitting fire, and the sound broke both my eardrums. Had I done as he had asked, we might have died on that mountain. This was a crazy man. I yelled obscenities at him and said I would never ever go hunting with him again. He was not just dangerous; he was insane.

When we reached the bottom of the mountain, we stopped at a bar to register the buck. I just sat quietly thinking that we were going to end up in jail. He had a head of a buck; how could he register a deer kill! Ken did not seem concerned because he had it disguised with the blanket. When the man came out to check the buck he complimented Ken on it and said he was certain this was the buck that half the county was after. It was a real trophy. The man never pulled the blanket back to look at the body that wasn't there. As we drove away, Ken said he was having this buck head mounted. He would show everyone what a great hunter he was. All I could think about was that he almost killed us. What would have happened to the children! It broke my heart to think about it.

The very next day Ken called the local newspaper and had his picture taken for the paper with his deer head. *What a phony*! I thought. He made up this big story about shooting this deer and dragging it for miles to the car. No one would ever know because I was the only other person there, and he knew I wouldn't say anything to ruin his triumph, his moment in the spotlight. What a liar and a phony. He told the story so many times he believed it himself.

Ken liked to party and spend money we didn't have. If he didn't have money, he would find some. Usually that meant pawning his diamond ring, his radio, or his rifle—whatever he could pawn to get a few dollars to play with. When I would find a pawn ticket, if I had any money, I would go retrieve whatever it was he had pawned and give it back to him. This happened at least two or three times. I don't know why I was so stupid. I guess I loved him so much that I could justify almost anything.

Ken was also a practical joker. He would do anything to play a joke on me. One day we had plans to go out in the evening. I was sitting on the floor with a hair dryer on the chair behind me, trying to dry my hair that I had set in hair curlers. The hair dryer was the kind that had the hood to sit under, like beauty salons use. My hair was auburn and very long, almost to my waist, so it took a long time to dry. Ken managed to get behind me and place dog poop on the air vent of the dryer. The air vent was behind me, so I didn't notice him do it. The heat warmed up the dog poop, and the smell slowly started seeping through the vents that were blowing the hot air on my hair. I didn't have a clue what was happening and thought one of the children or even Ken had walked through some dog poop, got it on their shoes, and had come in the house with it. When the smell got stronger and stronger and no one was in the room but me, I pushed the hair dryer away and discovered what Ken had done. I was angry to say the least because I had to rewash my hair and start over. Ken laughed so hard he was almost rolling on the floor. He told me to lighten up. He said he was just having fun and wanted to know why I couldn't take a joke!

This was not the first time he had played a joke on me. I told Ken that one day I would repay him for *all* the jokes he played on me and it would be the ultimate practical joke, so brilliant that it would only take one time to get even. He just laughed and said he wasn't afraid because he could take a joke, even if played on him.

Time was moving on with my pregnancy. I still had not told my parents. I was too embarrassed to tell them I had made a foolish mistake. How could I tell them I got pregnant! I knew the longer I waited to tell them the harder it would be, but

I just didn't have the courage. I was an adult now but was still afraid of what my parents might say. It was because I had total respect for them and did not ever want them to think poorly of me.

Ken suggested that since we were blessed with three healthy children, we should consider sharing by giving this unborn child up for adoption. He even had the perfect couple in mind. They had a child who was dying. The little girl was five years old and was no bigger than a one-year-old. I was told she would go into convulsions and they would have to push a button on the back of her neck that would bring her out of it.

I felt very bad for them; they were good, kind, and caring people. They could not have any more children and wanted a healthy child so much. They told me they would do anything if I would consider giving the child to them for adoption because their little girl was not going to live much longer and they had so much love to give a child. I must admit the thought of giving up our child to this couple was not so far fetched. Ken was right we were blessed with three children. I was not willing to commit, but did say I would think about it.

During the next couple of months Ken decided he was going to change professions, giving up tending bar and becoming a hairdresser. There was a big demand for men in the hair salon business. He decided he would go to school for cosmetology like two of the waitresses that he worked with in the bar.

The ladies were very nice and were our friends. We called them Nancy red and Nancy brown because they were both named Nancy and one had red hair and the other had brown hair. I am not even sure what their last names were. They went to school during the day and were cocktail waitresses in the evening. When they finished their training, they would be full-time hairdressers.

Ken figured if they could do it so could he, so he enrolled in class. I figured it was just a phase and he would soon get over it because I knew it was a lot harder than he thought it would be.

All of a sudden he started telling me I should pay more attention to my makeup and make myself look better. I told him if he knew so much, he should show me how to change it. He declined.

The next thing I knew, he was telling me to strengthen my chest muscles to enlarge my breasts. Place my right hand on my left wrist and my left hand on my right wrist and then pull and push. I looked at him with a blank stare. Where was this stuff coming from! Then he asked me to rearrange the dishes in the cabinets so that the ones I used the most were on the highest shelf and then when I reached for them I was to kick my leg out behind me as far as I could to stretch and tighten my butt muscles. I laughed at him. I said if I did that I would never get the cooking done and there was nothing wrong with my breasts or my butt. I wasn't a model, but I had three children with one more on the way. What did he expect of me! I only weighed 120 pounds, so surely I was not overweight.

Perhaps he just went to the classes because of the girls, I don't know. I trusted him and would never have believed he would cheat on me, so I pushed that idea out of my mind. I was right though; it only lasted a few weeks. He couldn't keep up with the studies and went back to just concentrating on tending bar.

I often thought I should suggest we go to Wisconsin to live, but I really loved the house and the neighborhood. Our neighbors across the street were George and Laura Talone. They had a son Andy. They were good people. George sang opera and had a beautiful voice. Laura was a lovely, pleasant lady who wouldn't say a bad word about anyone. The neighbors across the street on the west side of us were a family of four. Bert and Norma Boogaard had two daughters, Cindy and Gail. The girls were very nice and had good manners. Cindy was old enough to babysit and was good with the children.

We had many friends who would come and go. Several of the guys were stationed at Lemoore Naval Air Station a few miles away. There was Tony Wiegel, who had an El Camino truck that he called, The Load. Tony was very easygoing and was really good with the children. There was Tom Allison, who we called Big Al the Kiddies Pal. He must have been six foot three inches tall. The children used him like a jungle gym and climbed all over him. Big Al loved the kids. There was Wes Hastings, who was tall and had bright red hair and freckles. We called him Spots. There was Kurt, who was an all-around nice guy; we called him Boss. I am not sure what his last name was. There was Jerry Lynch, who was always laughing and joking. He was always fun to have around. These men became almost family to us because most of the time one or more of them stayed at our house. Sometimes on weekends they were all there. The children liked having them there because Ken was always happy when his friends were around.

The guys gave me the nickname Big G. At first I thought they were trying to say I was big, but then they explained that Big G stood for goodness, like the cereal. I was flattered.

Since money was tight, Ken decided to sell our station wagon and trade it in for something cheaper to run. What he bought was a blue convertible. It had a white top and white leather seats. I know it was an Oldsmobile, Delta 88, but I don't remember what year. I often wondered what he got for the station wagon because he never told me. Perhaps he stashed a few dollars for himself, but he told me it was a good deal. I really liked the car and so did the children. It was fun driving a convertible because it was very warm in Hanford—sometimes too warm!

As my pregnancy progressed, I stayed home a lot, and Ken ran with the guys. If he wasn't tending bar he was out drinking with the boys. I would get very upset sometimes because I never knew where they were going or what they were doing. But, as I said, I trusted Ken and could not imagine him not being faithful. I guess that is what love does to a person.

On many occasions they would get so drunk they would go on stealing binges. I never knew what they would come home with. We had wooden ducks, an old plow, and other yard ornaments they had taken from someone else's yard.

One morning I had to go to the store, and the guys were still asleep. I went to get in the car and saw straw sticking out of the trunk of the convertible. I was truly afraid to open the trunk for fear of what I might find. I went in the house and started screaming at Ken. I made him come out and open the trunk. It was a huge wagon wheel. I was furious. I knew I had to at least let them all know that I was furious with their stealing.

When I returned from the store, I woke everyone up with loud stereo music. I told every one of them I was not happy with their stealing and that it had to stop. If they wanted to steal they should take the stuff somewhere else; I would no longer tolerate their thefts. I explained that they were in the armed services and the government would protect them, but Ken was not, and he was the one who would get hung out to dry for these crimes.

What I didn't know was that they had stolen a whole ton of hay and the tarp that covered it and unloaded it in the field by our horses the night before. I found the hay and discovered what they had done when I went to see the horses that afternoon.

The Monday following that weekend, a detective showed up at our door. I was really spooked. Ken was home so I decided to let him handle it. I was certain the detective noticed how pale I became. Ken talked with the detective for almost a half hour and totally denied knowing anything about any stolen hay. The detective explained that the tarp we had covering the hay in our field was identical to the missing tarp that covered the missing hay. The detective noticed that we didn't have a truck and also knew we could not have put it in the car; although I am sure there was still some straw in the trunk, had he looked. Ken just said he bought the hay many months ago and the tarp came with the load. Ken told the detective that he had paid cash for the hay, didn't know the farmer's name, and didn't have a receipt. The detective said he might be back, and then he left. I was a nervous wreck. I told Ken I couldn't believe he put our family in that position and the stealing had to stop, immediately! I wanted him to give the hay back, but Ken said if he did that, he would be admitting guilt and would still be sent to jail. Nothing else ever came of it, I guess because they couldn't prove he took it. But the stealing did stop, at least for a while.

We had very little money, and we were living from month to month on my government check. Ken's money always went for parties and fun. Having a swimming pool brought lots of people over. Of course Ken liked to brag about the house, the horses, and the pool to people and would invite them over. Sometimes I didn't know what to do about dinner. The children needed to eat, but I didn't have enough food for all the other people. The guys would bring soda, beer, and groceries, but it was the strangers Ken brought home that I really didn't want there. Ken was always a gracious host and insisted I be gracious also, no matter what it took.

I am ashamed to admit there were some days I had to cash in coupons to get enough food for us to eat. The stores let customers cash in a maximum of one dollar worth and use the coupon money on other items. Customers didn't have to buy the products on the coupons. It was embarrassing, but sometimes a necessity. I would go back two or three times to different checkers so they wouldn't know I was cashing in more than one dollar's worth. I felt like I was stealing or cheating. But I had to do it because there was nothing left at the house to eat. I desperately wanted to leave what little money was left in the bank for the children.

The parties were never ending. Ken was popular, the joker of the group, the life of the party scene. He truly liked making foolish bets. Ken had a tattoo of a cock hanging by a noose that was placed just below his knee. Ken would bet people he was such a stud that he had a cock that hung below his knee. Of course they would always look at me, and I would have to say, "Yes, he has a cock hanging below his knee." He would make lots of money or free drinks on that bet. The women would giggle when he pretended he was going to drop his pants to show them, but as far as I know he never actually did, at least not when I was there. He would just pull up his pant leg to show the tattoo of the hanging cock.

He used me as a plant to bring up key words that would trigger his repertoire of jokes. One joke right after the other! He kept people laughing all night. When it became evident it was getting harder and harder for me to keep up, he told me to stay home. After all, I couldn't drink and I tired easily; therefore, I was no longer fun to be around. "Why should you go along and kill everyone's fun?" Ken would ask. He was all fun and games a lot of the time, but not twenty-four hours a day. I wondered if people actually knew that. We would argue about all the drinking and partying and my wanting it to stop so we could have a normal family life.

There were nights, or I should say mornings, when Ken was tending bar that he would telephone, giving me only moments' notice, and expect me to get out of bed to fix breakfast for three or four people at two o'clock in the morning. He told everyone I liked doing that for him and that I didn't care how many he would bring home; I was always cheerful and ready to serve, but deep down I was furious. He would tell them he was so proud of me and loved me for doing that for him. He knew I hated that, but he also knew I would do it and not embarrass him in front of his friends. It was unfair of him to ask me to cook at that hour and, worse yet, to treat other people to our groceries. The next day I would complain, and he would tell me to just get over it; we would manage.

I also learned early on that I was never allowed to return a drink in a bar if it was not what I ordered. He would tell me to drink it and shut up, that a bartender's job was not easy and he did not want me complaining. People make mistakes, and they correct them, but I was never allowed to speak up. I was also never allowed to complain about my food if it wasn't right at a restaurant. After all, cooks and waitresses work hard, too. Just smile and never complain. I always thought that it was stupid to eat or drink something that wasn't right or wasn't what you ordered. But only someone who knew Ken could understand how strongly he felt about that. So, I did as I was told. Thank heavens it didn't happen very often.

The farther I got into the pregnancy the more I knew there was no way I was giving up the baby. It was part of me and even though we were not married at the time, the baby was still part of the family. Ken was angry with me when I told him. He said we didn't need another responsibility. I told him if he cut out some of the partying and bringing people home, we could make it without a problem. I didn't care, the baby was mine, and I was keeping this child no matter what. This was my choice, not his. I had stood up for myself and was proud of it.

The couple that thought I might consider the adoption was very disappointed and unhappy, but they understood. They knew how hard it would have been. I was truly glad I had made the right decision, and I would stick by it no matter what. This little life was growing inside of me, and I loved it no matter what.

13
The Wedding

The second week of June in 1968, I had a doctor's appointment. The doctor said the baby was close, but it could be another week or more. I was unnerved at the thought of the baby being born on June twenty-seventh, my due date, because that day would have been my ninth wedding anniversary to Larry. I couldn't do that, it wasn't right. As the day grew closer I pleaded with the doctor to induce labor so it would not be born on that day. Of course, I couldn't tell Ken because then I was living in the past again.

The morning of June 26, the doctor gave me a pill to induce labor because he said I was ready. I later found out that the baby had decided on its own that this was the day because before the pill could take effect the labor started. Ken was scheduled to tend bar and could not find a replacement, so he said. He took me to the hospital, dropped me off, told me to call him, and went to work.

I couldn't believe it! This was my fourth child to deliver alone, without the baby's father by my side. Even though the delivery went well, I was still wondering why I always had to be alone for these major events in my life.

Little Cindy Lou was born on June 26, 1968. We would give her Ken's last name even though we were not married. What a beautiful little girl she was. I was ashamed of myself when I thought about having considered giving her up. She was perfect, with big eyes and blond hair. After I called Ken to tell him he had a daughter, he said the owner would take over for him at the bar for a short time. Ken came to visit for an hour—one hour, then he went back to work.

It was not until days later that I found out it was a scam that he couldn't get off work. He just didn't want to be there because he didn't like hospitals. At that point I didn't care, the delivery wasn't that bad. I had a lovely daughter, and the children were all happy they had a baby sister.

I was happy that I could get into my bikini. In fact, I filled it out better than before I was pregnant. I had only gained seven pounds throughout the pregnancy and felt truly good about myself.

I told Ken it was time we spoke about making a permanent commitment to not having any more children. I told him I would have my tubes tied; it was a simple procedure, and I would be in and out of the hospital quickly. Ken said no way. He said he wanted to make the sacrifice for me and he would get himself fixed. I was impressed that he would consider such a thing and agreed. However, every time I made an appointment for him, he either canceled it or refused to go.

It was September, and I knew Christmas was coming and we had no money for gifts for the children. Money was really tight now with the baby needing things. Ken said not to worry, that the children didn't need much and we could make it up to them when we were better off financially. I knew in my heart we would never be better off. I felt like I had let the children down by Ken continually spending money we didn't have. I was depressed, but how could I stop him? It is impossible to change people who don't want to be changed. The very thing I admired about him in the beginning of our relationship was now a nightmare.

A few days before Thanksgiving of 1968, the guys asked if I would cook a turkey dinner with all the trimmings, if they brought it. I said of course I would because I knew that otherwise we would not have much for the family for Thanksgiving.

Little did I know, they had been checking out a turkey farm and were planning to steal a turkey! I didn't actually see them steal the turkey, but I heard them laughing about the nighttime theft and how they almost got caught going over the fence with a live turkey in a sack. They killed and cleaned the turkey out in our backyard, and turkey feathers were everywhere. The bird was finally ready for me to cook. I was not impressed with the turkey heist but was grateful we had food on the table for everyone to enjoy. Even though it was another theft by the gang, it was, after all, Thanksgiving. I was hoping this would not trigger the theft ring again.

Ken kept working his mind games on me and with his charm convinced me it was time we got married. We had a baby girl together, and he said he did not want to lose his rights should I decide I didn't want him anymore. He worked really hard on the line that if I truly loved him I would make him an official member of the family so we would truly be a family. He wanted to end the year as my husband, so we planned a trip to Reno where we could get married without everyone in town knowing we were not already married. He promised me things would be different. He would be a good father, and he would not party as much.

What I didn't know is that he had been secretly gambling in town and really wanted to go to Reno to gamble. But I was in love and, of course, felt he wanted to be alone with me because we knew the wedding would be a brief getaway with no honeymoon. The trip was planned for a few days before Christmas.

He convinced me that we should really celebrate our wedding in style and I should take a thousand dollars out of my bank account in Long Beach to pay for the trip. I must have been really brain-dead to think this was right, knowing full well we were low on money. We were going to celebrate our wedding. Right! What was I thinking? To be honest I guess I wasn't thinking at all. I look back at all of this and hold my head down in shame.

On December 20, the guys had offered to stay at our house and watch the children while Ken and I went to Reno to get married. It was their wedding present to us, so we wouldn't have to pay a babysitter. How thoughtful! We trusted them because they truly cared about the children. I knew the children would be safe. Cindy was six months old now and no longer a tiny baby, so I wasn't worried.

On December 21, 1968, we landed in Reno, Nevada. I was excited about traveling and just plain getting away for a couple of days. Reno was lovely; I was in love and pictured a beautiful wedding day in a cute little chapel. I pictured us all dressed up, with flowers, and a honeymoon night, just the two of us.

Wrong! We got married at a Reno wedding chapel in our blue jeans as soon as we got there because Ken wanted to hurry up and gamble. No flowers, no singing, no candles, no nothing. It was a cute chapel, but that's as close to my vision as it came. He didn't even want to waste our time getting a room because he said we wouldn't be spending time in it anyway and it would be a waste of money. I insisted we at least have a room. He must have noticed how unhappy I was on our first day of married life and decided to give in. I went to the bathroom and cried. This is not what I had envisioned for my wedding day.

Ken didn't even notice I had been crying and rushed off to gamble. I decided what was done was done and not to mope about it. I walked around and looked at all the sights. It was impressive. All the lights and noise! I did a little shopping for the children, and then I found Ken at a blackjack table. He was not happy to see me and told me to go get my hair fixed or something because he didn't like me watching him; it was bad luck. Ken told me to come back in a couple of hours because he was going to own the place.

Why was I so dumb? How could I have allowed myself to be put in this position? I did as I was told and went to a beauty salon to get my hair fixed. After all, it was a treat for me, why not? Because my hair was so long, it took almost three hours. And it looked hilarious. It was teased to about three times the size of my head and curled upward on the ends. The spray was so thick my hair did not move at all and felt like a stiff brush on my head.

I was worried about Ken and rushed back to the table where he had been playing. He wasn't there. I went back to our room only to find him slumped in a chair. I asked what was wrong, and he said he was playing blackjack so well that he had increased our money up to nine thousand dollars when they changed dealers on him several times and he lost every penny back to the game. I just stared at him in sheer disbelief. He had done what? In three hours he had lost nine thousand dollars! Ken explained that he doubled down when he was losing because that's the way to change your luck. Obviously that didn't work for him. He said the dealer kept warning him to leave the table while he was ahead, but he was not going to be scared off. He was going to own the place, and the dealer was going to be working for him. I was speechless! What could I say about such stupidity?

Ken asked how much money I had left. I said not much, and I surely wasn't giving it to him. He suggested that we sell our airplane tickets for money to gamble with and that he would buy them back when he won. No way! I was not letting that happen. I had the tickets and a few dollars for food and taxi to the airport.

Our plane left the next day around noon, and we were going to be on that airplane. Thank God we paid for the room, or we would have been sleeping in the hotel lounge. I was just heartbroken. While he slept I stared out the window, wondering what I had gotten myself into. *Am I even actually married? What if his first wife never divorced him? I haven't seen any papers. He is just certain she has divorced him by now.* As I stared out the window, I wondered how my mom would deal with this! Then I told myself, *She would never have let herself get into this position to start with, but if she found herself in it, she would stiffen up and move forward with the attitude, I made my bed, now I can lie in it.* I made my choice no matter how wrong it was; now I was going to have to deal with it. I was so scared! Our conversation until we got home was very short and abrupt.

When we returned to Hanford, the children were happy to see us, and I was truly glad to see them and to be home. Actually, I was very glad we had a home to come home to. Ken was very attentive and gave the appearance of a happily married man. I, however, had huge reservations on that one. I barely spoke to Ken, and I think the guys noticed the tension between us because they congratulated us and left.

Late on Christmas Day, the guys showed up with presents for the children and food and drinks. It was really a nice Christmas even though we had bought very little for the kids ourselves. I was still depressed from the trip and wished I had never let him convince me to marry him. But wishing wasn't going to change it.

New Years came and went, and a new year began. The next few months Ken seemed to change, but not for the better. His temper was short, and he often had strange mood swings. Ken was restless, and I could tell something was bothering him, but he wouldn't tell me what. I feared maybe he was seeing other women because he became obsessed with where I was and with whom. It was strange that he became so paranoid after we got married. I assured him I wasn't seeing anyone. Why would I? The thought of his first wife cheating on him kept coming to my mind, but I knew there was no other man in my life, so I had nothing to hide.

Ken was still tending bar, and we got money from the government for the children, but my pay as a widow was cut off. We were a family now, and no matter what, I was just going to have to make this work.

One afternoon in early summer, Ken announced that he was going to become a professional gambler. "Gambling is where the money is," he said, "and if you handle it carefully, big money can be made." I was horrified. That's what was bothering him; he had become addicted to gambling. We were doomed! I told Ken that there was only big money in gambling, if you had big money to play with. Money makes money, and we were not even close to that level. He said he would start out small and when he reached the playing field with the big boys, he would be on top of the world. I thought to myself, *in prison is probably more like it*. I told Ken I would not help him become a professional gambler and that if that was really the career of his choice he would do it without the family because we would leave him. Ken immediately switched gears and said he was only testing me and merely wanted to see my reaction. I told him I was adamant about this, no gambling.

The very next week I found out just how determined he was. The title to the blue, Oldsmobile Delta 88 convertible was in my name, but he forged my name on the title, sold my car for two hundred dollars, and then lost the money in a poker game. We had no car.

It's like I'm in a soap opera or something. This just can't be happening to us. What next, the house? I wondered. Ken played the mind games on me again saying, "I am so sorry, and I know you can throw me out, but please give me another chance." He had a way of always making me feel guilty for his indiscretions and give in to his pleading for forgiveness. He played heavily on keeping the family together, saying that he loved me and the children, couldn't live without us, and didn't want to. It worked every time. I wanted this marriage to work because I didn't want the children to be without a father and I didn't want to be alone. But at what price was I hoping for happiness and a good family life? Was I ever going to have this with Ken?

The next month Tom Allison asked us to take care of his car while he was overseas. That was a blessing in disguise because we didn't have a car. I had guessed that Tom felt sorry for the family and it was his way of helping. He would have put it in storage anyway and this way it would be useful to someone. My marriage was on the rocks for months. I assumed Ken wasn't gambling any more, but I stopped buying back whatever he pawned from the pawnshop. It was only feeding his hunger to gamble. His mood swings had subsided, and he seemed his old self again.

One night we were sitting on the patio, just the two of us, talking quietly about nothing special. Ken asked what I would do if I caught one of the kids with drugs when they became teenagers. I told him I loved them and the best thing I could do for them was turn them in to the law enforcement officials. I was totally against drugs of any kind and hoped I could spare my children from the drug world. I thought it was a strange question and asked why he brought it up. His reply was that he was just curious. Now, is that not a red flag? To me it wasn't; I accepted his answer, and he changed the subject.

Ken then said he had a good idea. The old man who owned the cotton field behind our house had told Ken he thought I was a good-looking woman and Ken was lucky to have me for his wife. Ken suggested we get a divorce so that I could marry the old man. The guy was old (perhaps in his late seventies) and would die soon anyway, and then I would inherit the cotton farm because he had no relatives. "Big money," Ken said. Then we could get married again and live a good life. I just looked at him with a blank stare, the deer in the headlights stare. Ken laughed and said he was only kidding. He mumbled that I was taking everything so seriously and should lighten up. At the time, I quickly forgot about his comments, but wonder today if he wasn't serious and just checking to see how I would respond. After all, Ken was in it for the money. Anything for money! How low was that? Is that not a con man's way of thinking?

The parties continued, and Ken seemed to be drinking more and more. At least I thought that was what he was doing. It appeared he was on an alcohol high most of the time. With four children I couldn't keep up with the drinking and had no desire to do so. Many nights I just stayed home.

One day when I was cleaning our bedroom, I opened his jewelry box to see if his diamond ring was in there because I had not seen him wearing it. What I found were ten, tiny, little white pills. I had no idea what they were but knew if I asked I would get yelled at for snooping. I had this strange feeling that it was a drug of some kind that was not prescribed by a doctor. I had to know what they were and, for the next few days, checked them to count to see if they were all still there. They were! One night when he left to tend bar I checked again, and two of the pills were missing. I knew I had to ask him and brace myself for whatever was to come next. I wondered if that could have been why he had brought up the question about drugs. If that was true, he wasn't doing a very good job of hiding it from me.

I gathered up my courage, and, when the time seemed right, I asked Ken what the white pills were. He was very agitated with me but must have known I had figured it out already because he told me the truth. He said they were speed and he took one now and then to perk him up for tending bar. After all, it was a hard job and you had to be fast and good at it to make the owners money. He told me not to freak out on this and to just let it be. After all, he wasn't addicted and could take them or leave them. I told him to leave them, that he was good at what he did and did not need pills to make him work better. I told him to get them out of the house because I did not want them near the children. I told him I was standing my ground on this and would turn him in if I found them again. That same day the pills were gone. I don't know what he did with them, and, quite frankly, I didn't care. But I felt he had gotten the message, and I guess I expected the problem to just go away.

One Saturday night Ken came home from tending bar and partying into the wee hours of the morning and woke me out of a sound sleep. Ken was either so drunk or so high that he could not even stand up straight. He told me he loved me and that because he loved me, he someday wanted me to watch him make love to Nancy brown to experience a new sexual high. I was not only hurt, I was sick at the thought. I knew he was in another world, but what world was it? Not mine, that's for certain. How could he ask that of me!

That night I slept on the couch in the living room because, after that remark, I couldn't bear to be near him. I didn't actually sleep much because I cried most of the night. During the night I heard noises coming from our bedroom but refused to go check on him. I didn't care!

The next morning around noon, Ken got up and went to get clean socks and underwear from his dresser drawer only to find that everything in the drawer was wet. Apparently, he had gotten up in the night and urinated in his dresser. Poetic justice, I called it. At least it was his dresser and clothes and not mine. He was embarrassed that he had done that, and he asked me to never tell anyone. He even cleaned it up himself!

He got very quiet when I told him what he had asked of me. He apologized and said he couldn't be held responsible for what he said when he was drunk. He said he didn't mean it and that I should know better. I was really hurt, and it was going to take some major kissing up to me to smooth this one over.

I wondered if he was having an affair with Nancy brown. After all, she was good looking, unmarried, and trying to support her child. She was the very type of woman that Ken always felt sorry for. She was the type of woman he wanted to be a big brother to or savior for. He always wanted to have his shoulder ready to cry on. *What ever happened to helping those he loves? There are people in need in his own family! What am I, an old shoe? How can he be so kind to Nancy and so mean to me? What have I done to deserve this treatment?*

Once again the mind games began. It went something like this: why was I picking on poor Nancy brown? He wasn't having an affair and she was a good friend of ours, how could I think that of her? Was I that insecure that I had to believe something he said when he was drunk? Did I not love him enough to trust that he would never have asked me to do that if he was sober? It must have been the combination of speed and alcohol that made him act that way. There it was—the truth. He was not only drunk, but also high. Ken begged and pleaded for forgiveness, promising me he would never take speed again. He asked if I was ready to throw our marriage out the window because of one stupid mistake. If I truly wanted him to leave the house and move out, he would go. He understood how hurt I was, and he would understand if I didn't want him anymore because of it. I hated him when he played mind games on me; I folded like I always did. He knew how to twist the words to make me feel empty inside with the thought of being alone and without him. There was that magic spell again.

The drinking and partying continued. One Sunday afternoon he wanted to enter into a pool tournament in Selma. I knew he was good at playing pool, but I had never seen a tournament and wanted to go along. He said it was a beer bar and if I went along, I would have to drink beer. I said fine, whatever. When we got there it was a double tournament. On one side of the room was the men's tournament, and on the other side of the room was the women's tournament. They were all playing for trophies. I sat by the table on the men's side to watch Ken play.

The women were short one player and asked me to please play. I told them I had never played pool in my life and wouldn't know where to start. Ken thought it was funny and said I should play. I tried a couple of shots and thought, *I can do this*! After all, it was just for fun; I knew I would never win. The ladies I played against kept beating themselves by dropping the eight ball, and I made it to the last game for first and second place. Ken was furious! I could see it in his face because he was playing poorly in the men's tournament and lost out in the third round. I won the second place trophy and was beaming with excitement. Ken said I would never be a good pool player and had won by default. I didn't care what he said; I was happy. I placed the trophy on the mantel over the fireplace for everyone to see.

I guess Ken decided he had better show me how to play. From then on when we went out, Ken would show me how to hold the cue stick properly and would coach me on rail shots. When I got better at it, I became his partner in pool games.

14
The Move to Wisconsin

Zap, I was pregnant again. What happened to Ken getting fixed! He even had the nerve to blame me for not using birth control and to be angry with me. I reminded him that the responsibility wasn't mine alone and that he hadn't gotten himself fixed like he had promised. Then, out of the blue, he said he never had believed he was the father of either child. I told him he could get a test done anytime he wanted to verify it; I had nothing to hide. He dropped the conversation. Again he suggested an abortion, but I flatly refused and again said an abortion was not an option.

The bill collectors were coming to the house on a weekly basis and we were getting deeper and deeper into debt. I was horrified and embarrassed. I didn't know what we were going to do. I was afraid the next thing to go would be my beautiful house.

When the bill collectors came to the house carrying a briefcase or suitcase of any kind, Diana would run to answer the door and ask if they were moving in and would they like a beer. *What have I done? What kind of a life is this for the children? And now, I have number five on the way!* I thought.

I was sick with worry. Would we lose the house? I had lost everything else, except Ken, if that's any consolation. We had no car, and the bills were mounting. I had already felt like I was sinking in a hole, and now I was pregnant again. God help me! I prayed and prayed for answers to this situation.

My prayers were once again answered. I knew what I had to do. I had to go back to Wisconsin and get the children out of this environment. I would sell the house, pay the outstanding bills, move to Wisconsin, and begin a fresh life. When I told Ken about my plan to move back to Wisconsin, he objected saying it was too cold back in Wisconsin and that he hated winter. He shook his head no; this was not a good plan. I thought I would give it time to soak in. He knew full well we were sinking here.

Over the next couple of months I kept thinking about the retreat to Wisconsin. I just felt we would be safe there and that things would be different. But every time I brought up the subject Ken would veto the suggestion. I begged and pleaded with him trying to make him understand that we were in deep trouble with no other way out. If we lost the house, we would end up in an apartment with five children. We were in over our heads, struggling to get air. I told him I was tired of the bill collectors. We even owed money to Cindy, our babysitter, and couldn't pay her. I told Ken that he was going to have to talk to the very next bill collector who came to the house. Ken said he would deal with it. The problem was that they usually came when he was not home, so I ended up having to make excuses for why we couldn't pay the bills. Some of the bill collectors had already put a lien on the house.

One day a bill collector came to the house when Ken was home. I watched the pro in action. He told the bill collector we were trying very hard to pay our bills and gave the appearance of remorse and sadness. Ken told him that every month we would throw all the bills in a hat. Then we would draw one bill out of the hat and that bill would be paid. He told him that if he kept pestering us, we would not even put his bill in the hat. The bill collector said he understood we were trying to pay our bills and would check back with us in a month or two to see how we were doing. Then he left. I was awestruck at how smoothly Ken had pulled that off. What a con man! Ken actually had the bill collector feeling sorry for us. I guess his mind games worked on other people, too.

Our baby was due in early May, and I wanted to be settled in Wisconsin by then. It was getting close to Thanksgiving, and I was worried about the big move. Ken would still not budge about going to Wisconsin.

We shared Thanksgiving with our neighbors, George and Laura Talone. They provided a goose, which I cooked, and it was a nice day. While we were eating, I slipped and mentioned that we might not be there next year, which took our neighbors by surprise. George got very upset and asked why we were moving. Of course I couldn't say, "Because we can't pay our bills and are losing our house," so I merely said I was homesick for Wisconsin and my family back there. Ken glared at me for even bringing it up.

After the feast was over and everything was cleaned up, the children went outside to play. Ken asked me if going to Wisconsin was truly what I wanted to do. I said yes, it was, we needed to get out of California if we were going to survive as a family. I did not want to leave him, but I needed to get away from there. I was having my fifth child and felt I just couldn't live like that anymore. Ken said maybe I was right, and he would think about it.

The next week, two of the guys came to our house with a used, nonfunctional ejector seat from a jet plane strapped on the back of their truck. I was astounded. They said they saw a row of them and thought of Ken, so they had put it in the back of the truck and just drove off the base with it, without even being questioned. I don't know whether or not this was true, but here they were with this ejector seat. Ken was ecstatic; he loved it and envisioned making it a piece of furniture for our living room. I told them all they were crazy and would be arrested. I wanted no part of this theft, if it was indeed a theft. They put the seat in the garage and covered it up.

The next few months went by quickly. Too quickly! I was getting further and further along in my pregnancy and feared that if we didn't make a decision soon it would be too late for me to travel. I knew if we stayed there we were doomed. I was seven months pregnant, and Ken, sensing my frustration, finally agreed to move to Wisconsin. He asked me how I planned to make this big move. With my being so far along in the pregnancy, wasn't driving that far out of the question? The navy would no longer move me, and we didn't have much money.

Ken came up with a plan. I would have to give him power of attorney to sell the house, since the house was in my name only. I would take the last of the money out of the bank and use it for airplane tickets for the girls and I to fly back to Wisconsin. After he sold the house, he would rent a U-haul truck, pack up our furniture, and drive the truck to Wisconsin, with the two boys. I felt uneasy about his plan, but at this point what choice did I have!

I called Mom and Dad and asked if the girls and I could stay with them until we found an apartment. They were truly glad we were coming back to Wisconsin and said yes we could stay with them. I am sure they had reservations about us staying with them, but they knew we had to stay somewhere.

I was so afraid for Leary and Michael having to stay behind with Ken. I knew he would expect a lot from the two boys, but we didn't have enough money for tickets for all of us and it was going to be difficult enough for me to handle the girls. I hoped the boys would behave for Ken on the long trip. I prayed for them to be good and not give Ken a hard time.

Giving Ken power of attorney to sell the house was very spooky. I prayed and had to have faith that everything was going to be all right or I would never have been able to make the trip. I made a list of all the things Ken needed to take care of, like taking a treat to school for Michael's and Leary's classmates, getting the proper paperwork from the school when it was time, taking care of the electric and telephone disconnections, and so forth.

We did not tell the children what was going on until we were within a day or two of leaving. I took a treat to the school for all the children in Diana's class. Diana was nine years old at the time, and she was angry with me because she didn't want to leave her friends. I tried my best to explain that I wanted to be where I grew up and that she would like it there. I couldn't tell her it was because we would lose everything if we didn't leave. I hoped some day when she was older that she would understand why I had to do this. I knew it was scary for her to leave California and move to a state she knew nothing about. I also knew she would have to adjust just like the rest of us. Hopefully in time she would be happy that we had moved.

Leary and Michael didn't seem to mind one way or another. I guess they just didn't understand what this big move was all about.

Leaving Hanford was very hard. I loved that house. I had dreamed of so much more for my children. Instead, I was dragging them out of school to another state. I couldn't blame this all on Ken, after all, I allowed us to be put in the position, and I had to take some blame, too. I felt like an irresponsible mother who had failed her children.

I cried when I left the boys standing at the airport waving to us, and my heart was breaking. Leary was only seven years old, and Michael was only four. They were still my babies, and we had never been apart before. I truly hated leaving them behind, and they looked so sad, but I had to do this. I loved my boys and could only pray they would be safe. I think it was one of the hardest things I have ever had to do, looking at their sad little eyes as I left them behind.

On the airplane I tried to think of other things to keep me from being sad. I thought about my childhood and how simple life was then. I thought about my brother and my sister and how good it would be to see them again. My sister, whose name was Geraldine, went by the name Gerri for short. I decided since I was known as Geri in California, I would use the name Geri in Wisconsin too. It was short for Germaine and was easier to remember. It might be a little confusing, but we would manage.

On March 5, 1971, the girls and I landed in Milwaukee, Wisconsin. It was very cold, and there was so much snow. My dad picked us up at the airport and drove us to Sheboygan. When we arrived, the house was full of family. It was not only our homecoming, but also a celebration of my dad's birthday.

I was so relieved to be home. I prayed again for the safety of Leary and Michael and hoped Ken wasn't being too mean to them. After all, they were just little boys.

I had to get Diana enrolled in a school. Cindy was only two so I didn't have to worry about school for her. It was so cold, and I needed to get winter clothes for the girls. My family was very helpful, and Mom bought some material so I could sew some school clothes for Diana.

My mom sensed that I was worried about what was happening in Hanford and tried to convince me that it would all work itself out. After several weeks had gone by, Ken finally announced that he had sold the house. He told me he took a loss on it, but the deal was done, and they would be on their way soon.

A few days later a bill collector showed up at Mom and Dad's house looking for me. I was so embarrassed I could have crawled under the sofa. They tracked me down from California to Wisconsin. I explained to the man that my husband was on his way and I would contact them as soon as he got here to make arrangements for payment. Mom never said anything but I was certain she knew then why I had come back to Wisconsin.

I found an apartment on Wilson Avenue about three miles from Mom and Dad and got it ready for my family. I knew Ken would like it because it was only about a block and a half from a local tavern. The apartment was not large, but it was on the main floor and was across the street from a vacant lot. It didn't have a yard, but the children could always go over to the lot to play. I was just happy to get my family back together and was so excited it was finally going to happen. I was counting the days.

Years later, I heard from my old neighbors in California that Ken partied hardy and had one particularly wild time after I left Hanford. I guess I should have expected that. He left the boys with babysitters and just gave it one last big blast.

By the time Ken and the boys arrived in Wisconsin, it was very apparent that it had been a long haul. The boys were tired but safe and did not appear to be any worse for the wear. I guess they must have been too afraid to be anything but good on the trip. I was so happy to see them and promised we would never be apart again.

I was glad they were there, but I was also so upset when I saw what Ken had done. He had rented a small U-Haul truck and had only packed what he thought I should have. He had left behind all the beautiful wall hangings and knick-knacks. The people that bought the house must have been very happy with what he left them. I was just sick that he had left so many of my beautiful things. My brooms and dust mops, some of the dishes, and many toys were all left behind. None of those things meant anything to him. I noticed immediately that his deer head and the ejector seat had made the trip. When I asked why he had gotten such a small trailer, he said because the next larger size trailer was more money than he had left. And besides, what he left behind he felt we could replace anyway. He said he did the best he could and that I should be glad to have gotten what I did.

The story he gave me was that after the liens were paid from the outstanding bills, there wasn't much left. In fact, he said that he hadn't even paid all the disconnect fees and final bills for the utilities and we would still be getting those in the mail. Ken must have destroyed the final papers on the sale of the house because he didn't have them. He said the deal was done and, besides, the papers were no good to anyone anymore. I guess he didn't want me to see them because I would have figured out just how hard he did party. He always had an answer for everything. Maybe he had even gambled a lot of the money away.

Mom and Dad were not impressed with Ken. They could see what I could not: that he was concerned only for himself. But there would have been no point in saying that he was bad or evil or no good because I would not have listened. Mom and Dad did not want to interfere in my marriage, but they were truly concerned for me and the children.

Ken and I went shopping at a large local department store for baby things that we needed. The baby was due in only a few short weeks. I tripped on a piece of carpeting that had fallen off a table and caught myself by grabbing onto the table. My heart was racing because of the fear of falling. Ken asked what I was doing! I told him I almost fell and it scared me. Ken made the remark that I should have fallen because then we could have sued the store. When he saw how disgusted I was by his comment, I got the usual he-was-only-kidding remark and was chided for not having a sense of humor.

Every member of my family and all my old friends tried to help Ken find a job. He said he wasn't ready and that he wanted to be there for me when I had the baby because he wanted to help me out. After I had the baby and was rested, then he would start looking for a job.

Then Tony Wiegel came to visit us in Sheboygan. He was one of Ken's old gang from Hanford. Tony had gotten married and was now living in Racine in southern Wisconsin. It was really nice seeing him again. He was one of the guys who always felt like family to us. Ken and Tony planned to go fishing the next day.

And yes, of course, that was the day the baby decided to be born. The mind games began. Ken was not happy. He claimed that he may never get to spend time with his friend again and that all prospective fathers do at the hospital is just sit and wait! Was I going to make him stand beside me and watch me in such terrible pain when he knew he couldn't do anything for me? At that point I just wanted to get to the hospital. I didn't care who was or was not there; I just wanted to get it over with. I was terrified of the pain I knew I was about to have. Obviously so was Ken, so he dropped me off at the hospital and he and Tony went fishing. I know Tony didn't think much of Ken for doing that, but I am sure he wasn't surprised. Neither was I!

I was alone again. I gave birth to five children without a husband by my side. Was there something wrong with me? This was not a normal, everyday event. The birth of a child was supposed to be a blessed event with both parents sharing in the love and joy. Why was I always alone and in pain by myself! I had no comforting words, no hand to hold, nothing.

I had a baby girl. I named her Laura Lee after a singer. The name just seemed to fit. She was beautiful, and I had no regrets having her.

However, I had made up my mind that my body could not take anymore pregnancies and I had to do something about it while I was still in the hospital. I spoke with the doctor about getting my tubes tied. He said that he could tie my tubes, but he would need Ken's signature on the surgery form. When I told Ken, he flatly refused to sign the papers. No surgery he said. No, he would not help me do this!

Ken was petrified that I might die under the knife and that he would be saddled with five children. How is that for selfish? I tried to tell Ken I was not going to rely on him again and that my body just couldn't take any more pregnancies. He didn't care: no signature, no surgery.

I spoke with the doctor and explained that Ken wouldn't sign the papers. I told him I was tired both mentally and physically and begged him to do the surgery without Ken's signature. I told the doctor that if I got pregnant again I would kill myself and leave a note behind blaming him for not helping me. The doctor saw my anxiety and frustration, and perhaps he believed that I meant what I had said. He agreed to do the surgery without Ken's consent. The surgery went fine, and I was only in the hospital one extra day. Ken was nowhere to be found when I went under. But that was what I had expected. I didn't even care. I had to do this.

As time went by Ken became restless. He went from job to job. Family and friends were concerned about us. After all, we had five children, which was a big family. I was concerned about us because I did not want us to fall below the poverty line, which to me meant food stamps. How embarrassing it must be to go to a store and give them food stamps! I certainly felt empathy and compassion for anyone who had to do that.

Ken finally found a job working at a factory in Plymouth. They made lawnmowers and snowblowers. Ken was happy; I was happy; and finally everything seemed to be falling into place.

15
Payback for Practical Jokes

Ken had heard about a house in the country in Sheboygan Falls that was for rent. It was on old Highway 23, now County Highway C. It would be closer to his job. We went to look at it. It was a cute house with three bedrooms, a large living room, and a nice kitchen. It also had a full basement where we could put the toys for the children to play when the weather was bad. It was great, and we asked to rent it. The children would have to change schools again, but at least they wouldn't be so crowded, and they'd have a yard to play in. Everyone seemed truly happy that we were moving to the country.

We moved in, and to my surprise Ken had gotten rid of the ejector seat that had made it all the way from California. I didn't ask where it went because I did not wish to be held accountable if it surfaced and questions were asked.

The landlady lived right next door and watched the house every day. I don't know what she thought we were going to do with it. But she was concerned because we had so many children. In fact, one day, when I went over to pay her the rent money she asked why so many cars where at our house that previous Sunday. I stated that we had had a birthday party for one of the children. She said she hoped it didn't happen too often because we would have trouble with the septic system. I thought it strange that she was concerned with our visitors and their bathroom use, but I wrote it off as the concern of an elderly lady who had nothing better to do. We all seemed happy there, and I did my best to make it a home.

Ken bought the children a gas-powered go-cart. They loved that thing. The neighbor children would come over, and everyone would take turns driving it down the lane behind the house. The children seemed so happy, and the sound of laughter filled the air. They had new friends and a new home, and everything seemed right for a change. Had we finally reached the happily-ever-after family life I so desperately wanted for me and the children?

One day, we received a letter from the university medical center in California. They requested that we take Michael for a follow-up exam at University of Wisconsin (UW) Children's Hospital in Madison, and said they would forward all his records. They wanted him to go for a follow up to the heart surgery he had had as a baby so that he could be checked for scar tissue. So we made an appointment, and Michael and I took the trip.

Michael was full of questions on the ride to Madison and never seemed to stop talking. He was so full of life and was always smiling. There was one question he asked that I will never forget. He wanted to know if spiders pooped. I had to laugh, not at Michael, but at his unusual sense of being. I told Michael if spiders eat, then they must poop, just like people do. He was satisfied with that and went right into the next question.

Even Michael's teacher said he was always noticing things, such as the leaves changing color, before the other children did. Michael had a sense of life that reached out to the everyday things we all took for granted. I guess it was because he almost died that he was blessed with this gift from God.

After the exam, the doctor told me that Michael needed surgery. The scar tissue had grown and was starting to build up around his heart. The scar tissue needed to be removed. Michael was about six at that time and was strong enough to go through the surgery. They explained that there is always a risk when putting a child under, but the surgery itself was not complicated. The surgery was scheduled.

Again Michael and I made the trip to Madison. This time for a hospital stay. The surgery went fine. Ken chose not to join us, but I had resigned myself to the fact Ken hated hospitals and would stay away at any cost. Both Michael and I did just fine without him. Michael seemed very strong. Every day I would bring him some new little toy from the gift shop.

Everyone seemed to like Michael because he was always smiling and seemed like such a happy child. One incident I remember from his stay in the hospital was that he was allowed to get up and go down the hall to the playroom. Apparently one afternoon Michael had spilled his water in his room, so he walked down the hall to get a mop and then walked back to his room to clean it up. The nurse said that all she saw was a mop handle gliding past the desk when she captured Michael with it. They all chuckled about what a good boy he was.

The day before he was to be released, the doctors told me that they had discovered that one of Michael's lungs was not fully developed and had unusual scar tissue around it. This was very rare. In fact, I was told that Michael was among only five children in the world to have this condition. I was awestruck. Michael was a miracle baby and now this? They said his lung may or may not develop, but that he was doing just fine without it. They wanted to see him again in a few years for a follow up.

That winter it was my turn to be sick. I ended up with double pneumonia and was hospitalized. I was in the hospital for eleven days. I wanted out so badly I stuck the thermometer in water to cool it off so it appeared I did not have a fever. It was awful. I missed the children and was worried how they were all getting along without me. Everyone was kind and helped Ken with the children. But when the doctors finally released me, I was very glad to get home.

Things seemed to settle down for a while, and Ken would spend most weekends at the bar down the road. I think he spent more time there than he did at home. Sometimes I would try to keep up with him, but it got out of hand and the drinking was making me sick.

Ken started complaining about the job he had and wished he could do something else. Because I wanted him to be happy I asked what he wanted to do. I suggested going to a trade school to get training in a field he liked. I asked him if he could have any job he wanted, what was the one job he would be happy at. Ken said he had always dreamed of owning his own welding business. He was, after all, certified. The more we talked the more he envisioned a welding truck with all the equipment he needed to take his business to the farmers in the field. It seemed like a great idea. The farmers always had days of equipment down time when they had to take the equipment to a repair shop. This way he could drive into the field and repair the equipment on the spot. It sounded good to me. We talked more and more about it. I encouraged him, hoping he had finally found his dream job and a business of his own. I gave a sigh of relief, thinking he may have finally found his place in the working world.

The only question was would the bank buy into his idea for a loan to get started. We made an appointment with a loan officer and found out the bank would stand behind us on it. Ken was so happy. He found a truck, a 1968 GMC, and the welding equipment and arranged the truck to his liking.

The next step was to advertise. Ken tried talking to people, but it wasn't enough; we needed to advertise. We needed business cards and signs. I was excited about this and really had high hopes for the business to take off. Ken did a few welding jobs for one of our neighbors who had a farm, and that worked out fine.

The problem was that Ken lacked the drive necessary to make the business successful. The calls were sparse, and Ken's enthusiasm quickly dwindled. He seemed to lose his interest in the business and stayed home more and more. I tried my best to encourage him and keep him interested.

One day I was angry with him because he was lying on the couch watching TV. I said, "You have a business that's going to waste because you are lying here on the couch. Why not get out and put out your business cards? You could go visit farmers. Let them know you are available for welding jobs." It was a terrific idea; he just needed guidance, direction, and enthusiasm. I needed to keep pushing him out the door because, after all, we had payments to make.

Ken told me that some of the work he was called to do was more involved than he had anticipated. He confided in me that he was lacking confidence in his welding abilities because he was afraid one of his welds would break and would injure someone. What then? I told him he was not afraid when he was working for the navy and asked why he was now. Ken said that was different; if you screwed up someone else was behind you to fix it and you wouldn't get sued. With a business of your own, you are responsible. I thought it was a lousy excuse for not working at the business and wondered if he had some other reason for this sudden lack of confidence. If there was one, he wasn't telling me about it.

I tried to convince him to take a course at the local technical college to update his welding skills, but going back to school didn't interest him either. I think sometimes he spent days in the tavern because I wasn't there to lecture him. The business seemed to hang on by a thread, but it was still going.

Then our babysitter from Hanford came to visit. It was great having her there. Cindy was happy to see how the children had grown, and the visit was a mini vacation for her.

Ken asked to take her to the local tavern and wanted me to stay home. I raised an eyebrow at that, but I knew better than to argue with him and getting a sitter that late would have been impossible.

Cindy seemed very distant after that night, and I wondered if something didn't happen that she was afraid to talk about. I wondered if Ken mentally or sexually abused her in some way. It would have surprised me, but I knew he was very affectionate toward her. I think Cindy was a little afraid of Ken, too, and perhaps would not have come forward. She was only here a couple of days and, as I recall, left earlier than planned. I truly hoped my thoughts were unfounded. Only Cindy and Ken knew the truth.

One day Ken came home and announced that he found another place for us to live. This time the house was in Plymouth, just off of County Truck PP and on Pleasant View Road. It was an old farmhouse that was being remodeled. It had a fireplace in the middle of the dining room and living room and had red carpeting in the kitchen. The master bedroom was downstairs, but the rest of the bedrooms were upstairs. It seemed cold up there, but Ken said with the fireplace it would warm up. The children had to leave their friends again and enroll in another school! They were not happy, but did not dare to complain. Ken said we were moving to make a better life for the children. Right, even I knew better! It was always for him.

Ken's welding jobs were few and far between. My old friend Tom McCue offered to hire Ken as a handyman. Tom had his own carpentry business, and he could use some help. That way if Ken had a welding job, he could do that first and then go work for Tom. I thought that was a great idea. That way he could keep the business and still make the payments on the truck. Ken seemed happy with the job. He said he got along really well with Tom and was learning a lot about remodeling jobs. It seemed like Ken had settled into it. He came home in good spirits.

Our financial situation was a little better, and Ken decided it would be nice for us to buy a boat and trailer so we could have family outings in the summer months. Then we could spend more time as a family and take the children fishing, swimming, and boating. Why not! Ken was working steadily now. Something for the family would be good, and if we could spend more time as a family instead of in the taverns, I was all for it. I envisioned all of us being truly happy as a family for once. We had the right car to pull it, a 1968 Ford station wagon.

We went back to the bank and took out another loan separate from the business loan and bought a boat and trailer. It was an eighteen-foot fishing boat, but I don't remember what year it was.

Ken had found another bar to frequent that had a boat launch onto Long Lake. He liked the folks there so much he gave them his deer head to hang in their bar—the same deer head that made the trek from California! Actually, I was glad to see that part of my life go away.

As time went by, the children had adjusted to Plymouth and were making new friends in the neighborhood. The children seemed happy. We had a new boat. Ken seemed happy at his new job, and again everything seemed just fine with the world.

Leary and Michael had made friends with two boys their age that lived right around the corner. Their names were Todd and Terry Lisowe. The boys grew close. Todd was Leary's age, and Terry was Michael's age.

We got to know their parents Bob and Joan. They seemed like a nice family with a good home life, and it was just what I had hoped for the children. Joan worked at a local factory about a half mile east of their house. Bob was an over-the-road truck driver for a carton-making company out of Sheboygan.

One Sunday when we were planning to go to the lake with the boat, the children asked if Todd and Terry could go, too. We said sure and invited Bob and Joan and the boys to join us. It was fun and everyone had a good time.

As time went by, Joan and I became very good friends. In fact, as friends go, I considered her my best friend because I didn't associate much with the other neighbors and being a homemaker, didn't provide me with many opportunities to meet people. When Bob was on the road for work, which was often, Joan and the boys would come over for supper or we would just visit. It was truly nice to have a best friend. She was a good mother and had a nice house, and I felt comfortable around her.

When Bob was home, the four of us occasionally went out together to dance or to have dinner. They were truly a nice couple and seemed happy as a family. It was exactly what I had hoped our family looked like to others.

They were Catholic, and Bob was very strict about going to church every Saturday or Sunday, whichever worked out best. Most Sundays after church they went to Charlesburg to his parent's home. Bob came from a large family, and Sundays were reserved for returning to his mom and dad's house where his sisters, his brothers, and their families would meet. Joan often mentioned to me that she wished they didn't have to go every Sunday. So whenever I could I would ask them to join us if we were going to the lake with the boat.

Joan liked to golf, which I knew nothing about. She also played softball. The only thing I knew how to do was play pool. I wasn't the athletic type. She often wore short skirts or culottes and had a really nice figure. Sometimes I felt inferior, but I wasn't going to let that interfere with our friendship.

After a few months Ken's happiness with this new job wore thin and he started to stop for a few drinks after work every night. It seemed like the drinking was getting heavier and heavier. Once again he was starting to get edgy and had no patience with the children. It brought me flashbacks of California and the constant partying.

Tom McCue was concerned because he saw what was happening with Ken. Tom confided in me that Ken told him I never cooked and was a bad housekeeper and that was why he spent so much time in the tavern. Tom said he told Ken that he has been in my house and knew I was not a bad housekeeper. He said he also told Ken if he would come home for supper, instead of going to the bar after work, he would more than likely find a warm dinner waiting for him. I told Tom I didn't understand why Ken would say those things. I always made sure he had a warm meal no matter what time he came home. And I would take the center out of the roast so he would have the best of the meat. I was in tears, and Tom comforted me. He said Ken was just going through a stage and he would try to get him turned around. Tom asked that I not tell Ken about our conversation because he did not wish to be his enemy. I thanked Tom for caring but knew Ken's partying was more important than anything else. I told Tom that I loved Ken so much that I worshiped the ground he walked on and would do anything to make this marriage work. Tom said he would always be there for me no matter what; all I had to do was ask and he would help if he could.

One day Ken came to me and said that the three diamonds in his ring had been replaced with flawed ones. I asked how he knew. His reply was that he thought he would have a ring with a diamond in it made for each of the girls, as a surprise to me. When he took it to the jewelry store they told him the diamonds were flawed and not in good condition. The pawnshop in Hanford must have had a good laugh at Ken's expense.

I couldn't believe the story that Ken was trying to pass off this time. Having a ring made for each of the girls was not something on his priority list. I knew he was either trying to sell it or pawn it again for a few bucks. Sad, really sad! That story was just a little too far fetched, but I didn't care anymore about that ring. At one time it was special and meant something to me; that's why I bought it for him. Now it was just junk!

On occasion we would meet Tom and Liz McCue for Sunday breakfast. It was a special time for Liz to be away from their large family and a quiet moment for them by themselves. I felt like we were invading their personal time, but Ken just laughed at that and said who cares.

I remember one breakfast in particular because I was so embarrassed. Ken ordered a big breakfast, and I ordered a small one. After I finished my breakfast, I was still hungry, so when Ken pushed his plate away I asked for the rest of his hash brown potatoes. He snapped at me and said if you get fat I will leave you. Tom and Liz both looked at me and saw my discomfort. After that I wouldn't have eaten those potatoes even if I were starving. I was terribly embarrassed and told him what I thought of his comment when we were in the car heading for home. I got the usual I-was-only-kidding routine and was told to lighten up. But I was not taking it as a joke, and he could see that. When we got home he dropped me off and went to the tavern. So be it. I didn't want to be around him anyway.

Laura, our baby, was about three now. She was Ken's pride and joy. She could do no wrong. The other children could get in trouble, but not Laura, no matter what she did.

One day she was standing on the couch, and Ken sat down beside her and said to her that Daddy was cold. I guess Ken was hoping she would get the afghan and cover him up. Instead, Laura responded that nobody cared. I froze because I thought she would get swatted for being so flippant, but Ken just laughed and gave her a hug. That was rare. He didn't usually hug the children. I was truly hoping life would get better for us all. How many times did I have to wish and hope for that? How many times had I prayed for us to be a happy family? I had lost count.

Ken was still working for Tom but took a part-time job tending bar again. It was a place he wanted to be. Taverns were always full of laughter and jokes and music. I guess it was an escape for him. It was always full of people looking for a good time, and Ken was always there to provide the fun.

This was an era when streaking—running through a public area with no clothes on—was popular around the country. Ken asked Tom to help because he wanted to streak through the bar where he worked. He asked Tom to drive him to the bar where he worked. He would then strip down and run through the bar from the front door through to the back door where Tom was to pick him up again. The plan was that Ken would then get dressed and they would come in the front door to see how it went and if anyone had recognized him. I was in the bar having a drink, unaware what Ken had planned. Ken did streak through the bar, but all I saw was someone running out the back door and everyone laughing and screaming.

When Tom and Ken came in the bar everyone was talking about the streaking and that Tom and Ken had just missed all the fun. They apparently had not recognized Ken in his birthday suit.

Tom sat down beside me and told me it was Ken that had just run through the bar and, although I was not surprised, I was embarrassed that he would do something like that. I told Tom that if I had been him I would have "forgotten" to pick Ken up in the back and that because it was winter, he would have frozen his butt. Tom laughed. He had the greatest laugh. It was deep and hardy, and he made me feel good even if I was angry. I would always end up laughing with him. What a true friend he was.

Another time when Tom had joined us in the bar, Ken had been moody again. Tom could see that I was not happy. Tom and I were just talking about how paranoid Ken had become. I told Tom Ken would read any fresh car tracks in the driveway and badger me as to who had been there. It was like he thought I was having an affair behind his back. That constant questioning made me wonder what he was up to. Tom said I was probably overreacting and not to worry.

Ken had been playing pool and then came to stand behind us. Then out of the blue he asked me if I loved Tom—right in front of him. I was embarrassed and asked, "What are you doing, this is our friend." Ken kept talking about this subject and would not let up. He said there is a difference between loving someone and being in love with someone. You can love someone, but be in love with someone else. He kept on and on until I said yes, I loved Tom as a true friend, but I was in love with him, as my husband. I am not sure whether that was what he wanted to hear or not. Tom just shook his head because he knew Ken would never have stopped nagging me about it until I gave him an answer. After Ken had walked away, I told Tom, now he had seen for himself what a weird person Ken was becoming. Tom told me not to worry about it; he would talk to him at work.

We continued to spend a lot of time in the bar. The drinking was again taking its toll on me. Ken arranged for me, him, Bob, and Joan to go dancing. The bar he worked at was having live music. Todd and Terry were at their grandparent's house for the weekend so Bob and Joan were glad we asked them to join us. We got a babysitter for our kids and away we went. We truly had a good time, and all of us had more than our share to drink. When we got back to our house Ken asked Bob and Joan to stay to chat and have a few more drinks.

I told everyone I was tired and was going to bed. When my head hit the pillow, I was out like a light. When I awoke in the morning Bob was above the covers sleeping in my bed. I got very nervous about this arrangement and wondered where Ken and Joan were and where the children were. They surely shouldn't find us this way. I quickly got up and out of the bedroom. Thank the Lord the children were not up yet.

Ken and Joan were sleeping in the living room. Joan was on the couch, and Ken was on the floor. I had a whopping headache and made some coffee. Joan heard me in the kitchen and got up. I asked what had happened and why Bob was in my bed. She said Bob got tired and Ken said he should go sleep with me, not to worry that I was out like a light anyway. Joan said Bob had a bad back and was not about to sleep on the floor. Apparently Bob did what Ken said he should do, lie on the bed on top the covers.

I knew this was not right and confronted Ken when they left. He laughed and said, "Nothing happened, did it?" I said no of course not. Bob was on top the covers, and I was underneath. Ken said, "Well, then don't worry about it. It's no big deal." I scolded him and asked, "If the children had gotten up, what do you think that would have looked like?" Ken just waved his arm and said, "Well, they didn't. Why do you worry so much?"

My joker husband! I thought about all the practical jokes he played on me in California. On the airplane ride to Wisconsin I had had a brief vision of what I could do to repay him for all the pranks he had pulled on me. One chance was all I would get, so it had to be a good one. The thought came and went without much recognition because I was sad that day. But on this day, I remembered that plane ride and exactly what I had to do.

Every time Ken was to tend bar he would slip into a really hot tub of water up to his chin to relax all his muscles and, most of the time he would fall asleep. It was my job to wake him so he wouldn't be late.

On a Saturday I slipped off to the store and bought two large bottles of black clothes dye. The plan was that when he was asleep in the tub, I would pour the dye in and mix it gently. Then when he woke up, he would be black from the dye. It would not wash off so he would have to go out in public that way. I had heard that when people used dye to color clothes, if they didn't wear rubber gloves, the dye would color their skin. I had never heard of anyone getting sick or dying because of getting dye on her skin so I figured it was safe. This practical joke would pay him back for *all* the things he had done to me. Since he was fair-skinned and blond, the dye should hold pretty well. It scared me because I knew he would be furious, and I had to make certain I was out of reach when he woke up or I would be head first in the dye, too.

My opportunity finally arrived. We were going to meet some friends later in the bar, and he wanted to soak for a while. I was gracious and offered to fill the tub for him, making it as hot as I could within reason. This would also help the dye take hold. Ken thanked me, got into the tub, and asked that I wake him in an hour should he fall asleep.

Twenty-five minutes later I opened the door quietly, and sure enough he was asleep. I put on some rubber gloves and opened the bottles before I reentered the bathroom. I lowered the bottles into the tub as close to the water as possible so the dye would escape the bottles without making splashing noises. I swished the water gently to mix the dye with the bath water. Ken remained asleep.

I slipped out of the bathroom and quickly got rid of the bottles and rubber gloves. I was already dressed for the evening because I knew after putting that dye in the tub, I would have to leave in a hurry. The children were at a babysitter's house so I wasn't worried about them enduring his wrath when he awoke. I opened the bathroom door before I snuck out of the house to ensure that he would hear the phone ring. The phone was how I was going to wake him.

So far the plan was working well. When I arrived at the tavern I told several of our friends what I had done and asked that they protect me should he turn violent. Our friends were laughing so hard and said yes, they would protect me. After all they had all heard the stories of his jokes on me. I would have given anything to see his expression when the telephone rang and he opened his eyes to see the black water around him. The phone rang and rang without an answer. I wasn't expecting him to answer because I knew he would immediately jump out of the tub and into the shower to try to wash it off. I asked one of our friends to go check on him soon if we hadn't heard from him. After all, I meant no physical harm to him.

About fifteen minutes later the telephone rang, and all eyes turned to me. Sure enough it was Ken, and he was furious with me. I reminded him that he always told me to lighten up, that it was only in fun, and I asked where was his sense of humor now?

Ken arrived at the tavern and was very sullen and quiet. He was wearing a long-sleeved shirt with a turtleneck collar. He had his hands in his pants pockets. Ken asked the bartender for a beer. When he pulled his hands out of his pockets to pay for the beer the whole crowd burst into hysterical laughter. His hands were colored, and everyone knew the rest of his body was dyed, too.

I do not recommend anyone try this themselves. I am certain it could be dangerous, especially if it got in someone's eyes or was left on too long. It was only a matter of minutes before I called him, so he wasn't in the black dye for very long. I felt relatively safe doing it to Ken knowing his habits, but again it could be dangerous. But for my purpose, justice was served.

All our friends spoke with Ken and told him it was funny and that he deserved it. After a while Ken started laughing, too. Remember, Ken was always the life of the party and that day he most assuredly got all the attention, even though the laugh was on him. By the time the evening was over Ken was no longer upset with me. It took several weeks for the color to fade from his skin.

That very night we made a pack, no more practical jokes on each other. That was what I wanted in the first place. When people love each other, they laugh together, but do not do things to humiliate or cause pain to each other. To this day I still have people come up to me and remind me of that evening. They cannot believe I actually did that to Ken. I will bet he remembers it, too.

If I had any common sense I would never have believed anything Ken said from day one and would have gone on without him. But life had other plans for me. I was not proud of dying him black, but I had to make the harassment stop. I did that, and that's the part I am proud of.

16
Ultimate Betrayal

Because we lived on an old farm, we had a lot of grass to cut. Early in the summer of 1974, Ken bought a small, inexpensive riding lawn mower. He wanted me to learn how to use it, but I refused. That was his job. If I did it once, he would expect me to do it all the time, and I felt he had to help with work around the house, too. He was making innuendos like I can never know if something might happen to him and then I would have to know how to use it. I still refused. Little did I know his plan for the future was in progress!

In late August of 1974, Michael was scheduled to return to the UW Children's Hospital in Madison. This time the appointment was for a cardiac catheterization, a test to check the blood flow through his heart. He would need to be hospitalized for a few days. He would have to be anesthetized, so there was some risk involved.

Once again I was afraid for Michael. I worried about whether he could remain strong during the tests. I made Ken promise he would be there for us this time. He needed to be there not only for Michael, but also for me. I did not want to go through it alone. The waiting was hard enough, but the fear that takes over was sometimes overwhelming. I had been through this so many times, but this time I was truly afraid and insisted Ken be there. He said he would, but the appointment was a few weeks away, and he didn't want to worry about it now.

We still had warm weather and went for one more weekend of boating on Long Lake. Our neighbors Bob and Joan and their boys came with us. We truly had a nice time, and the kids had a lot of fun fishing and boating. I remember, in particular, one trip up and down the lake; Joan and I were sitting in the back enjoying the ride and the warm weather. She said that I was truly a friend and that she considered me her best friend. She took my hand and squeezed it. I felt good that I had a close friend, too, and returned the compliment. Ken wanted to know what we were talking about because we had been talking softly, and he could see we were getting emotional. I said we were merely talking about the nice day and how much fun it was to share it with good friends.

The next day I had to get the car checked out, and Joan gave me a ride to the mechanic's garage. During the ride Joan confided in me that she was afraid of Bob when he had been drinking a lot. She said he would get jealous of whomever she had talked to and then would grill her about them. She went on to say that one night she threatened to leave him and when she went into the bedroom to get some things, he lay outside of the bedroom door and wouldn't let her out because he didn't want her to leave. She said she felt like a prisoner in her own home. She asked how Ken treated me. I said he was moody but never lifted a hand at me in anger. I told her about Juanita and his son little Ken. I told her about the attempted murder charge, but that it was dismissed. I said Ken was always the life of the party and lived for fun and laughter. She said she envied me for having someone around who was fun. I told her Ken was fun, but not fun twenty-four hours a day and the drinking was, many times, too much for me to keep up with.

The next week Ken and I started arguing constantly about anything and everything. I spent most of my time in tears. I wanted so much to please him, yet nothing I did was good enough.

One night I was to meet him at the bar where he worked. For some unknown reason I took a different route to the bar, and, as luck would have it, I got a flat tire. I called the bar and asked Ken to come fix the tire. When I told him what road I was on, he was furious. He made insinuations that I was having an affair because I never take that road. There must be a reason; a boyfriend lives on that road. He accused me of cheating on him. I thought he had lost his mind because I had no interest in anyone else.

I pleaded with Ken for us to get help to save our marriage. I wanted to see a marriage counselor or someone who could help sort out our differences! Ken admitted we had a problem, but said that he did not wish to air our dirty laundry, so to speak. He said the problem was with him, and he was going to deal with it to make things better for us. He said he would make arrangements soon to make a better life for us and that I should just be patient. I was proud of him not only for admitting we had a problem, but also for admitting he was part of the problem. It was astounding. I sensed personal relief as if everything was going to be right again; I just had to give it time.

Ken told me it was time to move again. He had been told this house was going to be sold, and he didn't want to get stuck moving in the winter. There was a farmhouse owned by his boss, the bar owner, that was for rent on County Trunk ZZ. It was high on a hill, but still in Plymouth so the kids would not have to change schools. Ken gave notice that we would be moving on October 1. Neither the children nor I were happy that we were leaving our good neighbor friends, but it was still in the area and we could still visit. We all hated moving time after time, and I hoped this would be the last time.

At the end of August, we made arrangements for me to go to Madison with Michael. Ken would come to Madison that night with the truck after he got off work. Because the test on Michael was scheduled for the next day, these arrangements worked out well. My best friend, Joan, would watch the other four children while Ken was in Madison with me. I was confident everything was taken care of, and Michael and I left for Madison.

Michael was admitted to the hospital and routine tests were taken in preparation for the big test the next day. As the hours went by, I waited patiently for Ken's arrival. It was getting later and later and still no Ken. Morning arrived, and Michael was asking where his dad was. I said I was sure he would be along soon and maybe he had had trouble with the truck. However, I was very worried because he should have been there already. Michael sent me out to the parking lot three times to look for his dad. He wanted to see him before they gave him the shot to put him under for the test. But, Ken was not there. By now I was upset, but I couldn't let Michael know. I had to pretend for his sake that everything was all right.

When they took Michael down for the test, the doctor told me Michael would not be back from intensive care for about four hours. I immediately headed for a telephone and called home. Diana answered the telephone. I asked her if her dad had any trouble with the truck. I didn't want to scare her either. She said he left last night. She said he packed what seemed like a lot of things in the truck, like the stereo, saying it was for me and Michael at the hospital. She said he told her to be a good girl and watch the children and that I would be calling her soon. Then he left. I asked where Joan was! Diana said Joan never came over and that she had been babysitting the other children herself. Diana's voice was shaky as she asked if everything was all right with Michael. I said everything was fine and I would call her later.

I immediately telephoned Joan's house, and no one answered. I tried for two hours, and finally Bob answered the telephone. He hesitated to speak to me, so I knew something was wrong. By now I was very upset and begged him to tell me what had happened. I was certain Ken was in an accident because he promised he would be there. I told Bob he needed to tell me no matter what, I couldn't stay there and just wonder.

Bob said I should brace myself and that he was sorry he had to give me bad news over the telephone, but Joan and Ken had run off together. I know I must have sounded dumbfounded, but I said I didn't believe it and asked how he knew. Bob said Joan had taken Todd and Terry to a babysitter and told the sitter that he (Bob) would be there the next day to get them. She left him a note telling him where the boys were. The note also said she was leaving with Ken because he said he loved her and would never hurt her. The note went on to say that she loved the boys very much, but that she knew if she took them Bob would continually hunt them down. She was taking the station wagon and her clothes because she deserved that much.

Joan must have made one of the hardest decisions she ever had to make when she decided to walk away from her children. She was a good mom, but I could almost hear Ken saying to her, "If you take your two boys, I will take my two girls, and how far will we get with four children?"

I was in tears and crying on the telephone. I told Bob I couldn't believe all this. I couldn't believe they left my children alone all night and took hers to a sitter. What kind of best friend would do that? She ran off with my husband, she was no best friend of mine. I was shattered. Bob said he was sorry and wished he could be telling me something else. I told Bob to hang in there and I would do what I had to from my end. Bob said he told his boys their mother went to visit an aunt in another state but would be back in a few weeks. I told Bob there was no point in lying; I would tell my children the truth.

I telephoned my parents and asked them to go get the children because Michael was not out of the test yet and I couldn't leave. I was honest and told them what I had just heard. My main concern now was the children. I told them I would get back as soon as I knew Michael was going to be all right. Mom and Dad said they would go right away and keep the children with them until I got back.

The next call I made was to Tom and Liz McCue. I explained what had happened. They were very sympathetic and said they were coming to Madison to be with me in my time of need. Now, these were good friends.

They came to Madison and took me out to dinner. The restaurant was just across the street from the hospital, and I wouldn't be gone long. During dinner Tom told me Ken had asked him for a two-hundred-dollar loan just two nights before. Tom said Ken told him I needed it in Madison, so he had given it to him. I told Tom I was sorry and didn't know what to say. If I ever got out of debt I would repay him. Tom said not to worry; it was Ken's debt not mine. Tom said he also heard that Ken borrowed the same amount of money from another friend of ours, Dale Carpenter, under the same guise and that Dale had given it to him as well. I was devastated, what a con artist he was.

After Tom and Liz left, I went to the chapel and prayed. I was so empty inside, like someone had ripped my heart out. I prayed Michael would be all right and be healthy enough to go home soon. I prayed for guidance and help for whatever was facing me now. I had to be strong and deal with the situation. Once again the burden of how cruel life can be was weighing heavily on my mind.

Part of my prayer was answered rather quickly. Michael came out of surgery sleepy but fine. I told him to rest and that I would be back to get him as soon as I knew when he would be released, then, I headed for home. I was thirty-four years old, and once again the children and I were facing the world alone. Only, this time, I had five children.

When I got home I immediately checked the drawer where we kept the blank checks, since I had the checkbook with me. Three packs of checks were missing. I called the bank and told them to close the account, but I was told the account was empty. Ken had taken whatever cash was left in the account.

So Ken had run off with my best friend, while Michael's life might have been in danger. I remembered Michael had sent me out to the parking lot three times to look for his dad. Ken left the other four children unsupervised overnight, borrowed money from our friends, took the truck and stereo, and cleaned out our checking account. Oh yes, and we were about to move.

This was what he had been planning all along. This was what he was going to do to fix things, to make things better for us. This was why he wanted me to learn how to use the riding lawnmower and why he accused me of having an affair. In his mind he was justifying leaving us. I sat on the bed and wept. Why hadn't I seen this coming! Why was life so hard so often?

As soon as I could get myself composed I telephoned Mom to let them know I was home and that Michael was all right. Mom said they would bring the children home to me. When they arrived they gave me a hug and stated they did not want to stay to see the children upset when I told them. If I needed them, all I had to do was call. I told Mom I was going to tell the children the truth. Then Mom and Dad left.

I sat on the bed and called Diana who was twelve, Leary who was eleven, Cindy who was six, and Laura who was three into the bedroom. They sensed something was wrong because I was already crying. I told them the truth; their dad had run away with Todd and Terry's mom. I explained that Joan took the boys to a sitter and then they left. I told Diana that is why I called because he never showed up. I didn't want her to worry, that's why I didn't tell her then that he hadn't arrived. It was also why grandma and grandpa came to get them.

I told Diana I was very proud of her for taking such good care of her brother and sisters after Dad left. Diana started crying the loudest and saying how could he do this to us, especially since he knew what happened to our first dad? How could he be so cruel to hurt us again? Didn't he love us? Leary asked if I was sure and how did I know. I tried to calm the tears by saying people do strange things and I can't explain it. I assured them that he loved them, that he just had to do what he had to do, and that it was probably me that he didn't love anymore. Diana and Leary were the oldest and, therefore, understood some of what was going on. They took it the hardest. They said they were going to hate him. They were going to hate him for the rest of their lives for hurting all of us. I guess in my heart, at the time, I hated him, too. I felt Cindy and Laura were maybe only crying because the rest of us were crying. They were too young to understand the depth of what had happened. I tried to explain to them that all I knew was Joan had left Bob a note saying she and Dad were leaving together, but I told them not to worry and we would be all right. The main thing was that Michael passed the test. He would be home soon, and we would manage. I said out loud, "I know the Lord will help us, and I thank the Lord for that."

I was angry, hurt, lonely, and scared. I had five children, no job training of any kind, and had to move in a few weeks. My name was on the loans for the business and the boat! How would I pay for them! I had no money; he took everything that was left. At least I had the boat and could sell it toward the loan, but he took the truck.

God help me, I prayed! I thought about Larry dying and how I got through that. I knew I would get through this, too, with God's help. I had my children, and I knew I would have to toughen up for their sake. I also knew God would not let me down, and he would help show me the way.

Would Ken's boss even allow me to move into the other house now that Ken wasn't there? I had to move, so I decided I better go, be honest again, and explain what had happened. I gathered up my courage and went to see him. I told him my dilemma and asked if they would trust me to move into their house up on the hill. He said yes and even offered me Ken's bartending job. I had never tended bar and knew nothing about it, but I was assured if Ken could do it so could I. So I took them up on their offer and said I would sure give it a try.

I went to see Bob to see how he was holding up. Bob was having difficulty with the laundry and the grocery shopping. I told Bob I was having trouble with vehicle repair, grass cutting, and moving and suggested perhaps we could help each other. I told him I would watch the boys so he could get back to work in exchange for helping me move and doing some of the manly things around the house. Bob agreed that would be good. Then he could get back to work truck driving. After all, the kids all got along great. It wouldn't be any more of a chore for me to have seven children than it was to have five. Even the children liked this idea.

The next week the welding truck was found. Apparently Ken drove it several miles away and then left it. I guess he knew someone would report it and I would get it back. If he had left with Joan, the children would have seen him, so he needed to be seen leaving with the truck. Well that was a relief. Apparently they drove away together in Joan's station wagon. Bob had made reference to reporting the car stolen so he would get it back, but he had reservations about it. I guess he decided she could have the car since she walked away from everything else. His two sons were his main concern, and he had custody of them.

My next step was the bank loans. I went to the bank and was honest about my situation. I told them I would sell the truck and the boat for whatever I could get and I would be responsible for the payment of the rest of the note. The folks at the bank appreciated my honesty and said they would help me sell the truck and boat and would make every effort to help me along the way.

Thank you, God, I prayed. Everything was falling into place, and my prayers had been answered again. The children and I were going to be just fine. It would be a struggle, but we would make it. Actually the children and I were closer than ever, and we pulled together to be the family we always wanted to be.

Many times I thought about Ken. I was totally convinced that he never loved Joan. He needed to run and he needed someone to run with. Ken never liked being alone. Joan was very vulnerable, and she fell under the spell of Ken's mind games. I am certain he convinced her they would both be happier if they left. He may even have convinced her that Bob and I were having an affair. After all, he had Bob sleep in my bed. She was justified then to leave. If she ever wanted to get away from Bob, this was the time and leaving was all right. Ken knew how to get the words twisted around just right so that he was always convincing and people would believe him.

I took an advance on my bartending check to make ends meet. The move went smoothly. Bob recruited some of his friends to help with the move, and Tom McCue came over to help as well. I was so grateful. The children were a big help and did what they could to get organized. Well, children and moving aren't a great match; they played more than worked, but I didn't care. We were all together and healthy, and that was all that was important. Life would be OK as long as we stuck together.

The next step for me was to file for a divorce. I needed to be free of Ken once and for all. I went to court and received my freedom. The divorce would be final on March 21, 1975. That marriage lasted seven years. I had endured seven years of mental abuse, and I would finally be free from it.

The next few months flew by quickly and every time I turned around or the telephone rang, I expected it to be Ken. There was always something in the back of my mind saying that he would return. What would I do? I had to have a plan in case this happened. I could no longer let him return to our lives. I could not let him play his mind games on me ever again. We were happy without him. In fact he did us a huge favor by leaving. Life was better, and the children seemed more content. I made up my mind I would just say no he was not welcome in our family. Of course that's easy talk for someone who folded every time he begged or pleaded for forgiveness, which was often. I tried to push the thought from my mind. After all, I was divorced now and owed him nothing. If anything, he owed me for paying the bills and for child support.

I don't know when Bob went to court, but I know he filed for divorce as well.

One night I had just finished tending bar and was having a drink when a man whom I had never seen before came in the door and came directly up to me.

"Are you Geri?" he asked.

"Yes I am," I replied.

"Would you ever take Ken back if he asked to come back into your life?" he questioned.

I felt like this stranger was intruding on my personal life and immediately said, "No."

"Why?" he asked.

"Not that it is any of your business, but he did us a favor by leaving. He went from job to job and was never happy. He spent money like it was water, was mentally abusive to me, physically abusive to the children, and no, I wouldn't take him back."

I turned away, and when I turned around again the man was gone. I never gave it a second thought at the time, but now I wonder if Ken hadn't sent this man in and was outside waiting for my answer to see if he should reappear. What if I had said yes?

Thank you, Lord, for giving me the right words. I just couldn't take any more of that life. I had to start anew. All I ever wanted was to be happy and to be at peace.

That he might be back was a scary thought. After he left, I heard various rumors about his many girlfriends and his drug-selling escapades. I was told he was the local drug dealer. I don't know if these rumors were true, but after the pill incident in California and the Nancy brown event, none of it would have surprised me. But if he was indeed a dealer, I was not aware of it. It certainly would have explained his mood changes and party-hard attitude. As for the girlfriends, I guess that was why he was always suspicious of me. He was cheating on me and was hoping I was, too, so he could justify his own actions. The sad part was that I had loved him so much that if everyone had told me bad things about him, I would have called them all liars. After having been hurt so badly I was not certain I would ever love that deeply again, ever.

17
Renewing My Faith

Over the next few months, I spent a lot of time in the bar. The children were getting annoyed that I was gone all the time. I tried to explain that I needed to work now and this was all I knew how to do. But they were used to having me home, and now it was different.

I woke up with headaches and became short-tempered and edgy. The children often complained. They felt like I was doing the same thing I had been irritated with Ken for doing. They were right. So young, yet so perceptive! I was falling into the same drinking pattern that Ken had been in.

I knew I had to make some more changes in my life and that I could not continue to drink the way I had been. There were nights that I didn't even remember driving home or even how I got home, for that matter. I began to feel like I was on the brink of becoming an alcoholic. But I told myself I needed to have some fun. Besides, drowning my sorrows in alcohol seemed to help. It was an excuse, of course, to validate what I had become.

Taking care of two households and seven children and working part-time was taking its toll on me; I was relying on alcohol to keep me sane. But, I was actually running myself into the ground. Alcohol was not a cure at all.

I asked several people that I respected whom they would recommend I speak to. I needed new guidance to get me off this track of destruction. I was looking for a minister or priest, someone who would not judge me but would help guide me. It was God who had to send me in the right direction; it was God who was always there for me. I had to find him again. Several of my friends recommended that I go to a Catholic church because it was always easy to speak to a priest. I asked for an appointment with a priest at the church that Bob and the boys attended.

I was amazed by the new outlook the visits gave me. There were no judgments, just compassion and understanding. The priest told me God would not want me to be feeling sorry for myself. He had given me the gift of life and was trying to show me the way.

I guess this was a big turning point in my life. I knew then my purpose on this earth was to write a book about the hardships I had endured and survived. With God's help, I would succeed and my story would be told.

At this point, I decided to take confirmation instructions to become Catholic. I never was concerned about confession. I would tell the priest who I was and what I was feeling repentant about. I never once felt intimidated by that. I didn't care what they knew about me, after all, they knew everything already. It was like a big boulder was lifted from my shoulders.

I felt like a better person, and I enrolled in Lakeshore Technical College in Cleveland, Wisconsin, to pursue a career. If I was to get away from the bar scene I needed a new path. I became a full-time student in September of 1976. At this point in my life any career was better than tending bar, and the priest encouraged me to take this step. My field of study was Materials Management.

It had been a long time since I was in school, but I knew it was the right thing to do. It was rewarding not only for me but also for my children. They would see the strength and courage I had to continue in life. It is never too late to try to better yourself. Never to late to get a better education! I had hoped it would give my children strength and courage as adults no matter what happened to them—the kind of strength my mom had instilled in me but that I had lost for a short time.

On my first day as a college student, I wanted desperately to blend in, even though I knew I was much older than the rest of the students. Most of the students were right out of high school, and I was thirty-five. I wasn't going to let my age be a factor in getting a higher education. Between classes I went to the cafeteria and to buy myself lunch. I had put my books on a table but had taken my purse with me to the counter. The purse had a shoulder strap, and I had it on my left shoulder. After I bought my lunch, I carried my soda and my hot dog back to my table. When I got there I leaned over to set the soda down and my purse slid off my shoulder very rapidly knocking the hot dog out of my hand. It went flying through the air and landed upside down on the floor in front of me. All eyes were on me. So much for trying to be inconspicuous! I guess I could say that moment was the most embarrassing moment of my life. But I cleaned up the mess and went without lunch that day. I knew if I got through that day I could get through the rest of school with a breeze.

Bob and I had helped each other for two years and had become close. We started dating, and all nine of us went to church together. On Sundays we went to Bob's parent's house like Bob's family used to do when Joan was there. I didn't mind it, though. Everyone was very pleasant to me and the children, and we enjoyed the visits. It was the family life I had always dreamed about for my children.

Occasionally Bob and I spoke privately about Joan and Ken and our lives with them. I told Bob what Joan had told me about her being afraid of him at times and that she had told me about the incident in which Bob was blocking the bedroom door. Bob said he always became more jealous when he had been drinking but never intended to harm her in any way. He loved her and just didn't want to lose her or his family.

Bob told me Joan had had an affair and he had found out about it. At the time the man worked with her at the factory, and Bob knew him and his family. Bob said he continually asked Joan to stop. He asked her to think about what she was doing and how many people would be hurt by her actions. He begged her to please end it. Joan always promised she would, but it didn't happen. Bob said he couldn't take it any more, so one day he took Joan to the man's house and confronted them in front of the man's wife. They agreed it was wrong and it would end. None of them wanted to hurt their families.

Things seemed good for a short time, but when he would call her from another state, she was never home. Bob again became suspicious that either she was at it again or there was someone new. So, when he was home he watched her very carefully. Every time she smiled at someone he would wonder if this was the new man in her life. Bob admitted it was taking a toll on their marriage. Joan was very defensive and resented Bob's accusations. The night he blocked the bedroom door was one of those nights when they had argued about Bob's jealousy and she had threatened to leave him. He made sure she couldn't leave hoping things would be better in the morning. He said in his heart he knew someday she would follow through with the threat. He had no idea that it would be with Ken, though, since he had seen nothing to indicate their attraction to each other.

I told Bob about my life with Ken and the one time I actually thought there was something going on between Ken and Joan. Ken had left the house to go tend bar. Joan was at my house with the boys. She said she wasn't feeling well and asked if I would watch the boys for a short time so she could rest. I said certainly; after all, she was my best friend.

The children were all outside playing when one of them came in and said they had seen Joan drive away toward town. I was surprised and tried to call her. Sure enough no answer. I thought it strange and wanted to ask Ken what he thought. I called the bar and was told Ken wasn't working that night. A huge red flag came up. I was actually sick to my stomach with the thoughts I was having. I had made up my mind I would be strong and would confront Ken about his lie about working and the fact that Joan was also missing.

When he came home I raised all the nerves I had in my body and asked how work went. He lied and said fine. Then I told him I had called the bar and found out he wasn't even working that night. Ken became furious that I was checking up on him and wanted to know what I was thinking by embarrassing him like that. Now they would make jokes in the bar about my checking up on him. Yes, once again the mind games began, and he turned the whole thing around to make it look like I was the one who had made the mistake.

I figured that since I already had him angry I might as well continue. So I explained what had happened with Joan. He jumped off the chair and asked if I was actually accusing him of having an affair with Joan. I told him it sure looked strange and asked him what he would think if he were in my position! Ken immediately went to the telephone and called Joan. He told her to come over because I had something to say that she needed to hear.

When Joan arrived I said I wasn't accusing anyone of anything but that I wanted them to see how it appeared. Joan stated that I must be kidding and that she merely went to get gas for the car and wasn't even gone very long. Ken jumped in and said he was working on a surprise for me and now I had ruined it. I didn't say much more, but I watched them squirm with their excuses. I wasn't sure what had actually happened, but if they had met somewhere, it was brief and hopefully I had shocked them into knowing I was not afraid to confront them.

The next few weeks Ken was very attentive, and we didn't even see Joan. He never did say what the surprise was for me. I guess he was just doing a good job of covering his butt, and she was too embarrassed to come see her best friend.

Bob was very surprised to hear that story; he had had no idea. I laughed and said maybe Ken's surprise to me was that he was leaving me and taking Joan with him. I told Bob I didn't understand why Ken wanted to hurt the one person who tried to give him everything he ever wanted. I didn't believe he loved Joan, but I did believe he would never have left alone, that he needed someone to go with him. She was vulnerable, and he played the mind games on her.

I had heard there were at least two other married women that he had tried to convince to run away with him. He was looking for someone who needed him, too—someone he could justify running with. Bob was speechless.

Over the years there had been no contact whatsoever from Joan and Ken—no calls; no cards, not even for any of the children's birthdays; no nothing. I knew at a minimum Joan had to think about the birthdays and holidays that she was missing. I am sure she often wondered whether running away had been worth it: not being with her children when they needed her; not being there for their big events at school and church; and missing all the scraps and bruises a mother's comfort could have cured. She missed a lot.

Christmas of 1976 was soon to be upon us. All nine of us sat down as a family and took a vote to determine which house we would have Christmas at. That was not a difficult decision. Bob had a nice house, and we all agreed to have Christmas at Bob's house.

That winter there was a terrible ice storm, and the power was off for days. We happened to be at Bob's house at the time, and we made the best of it. I cooked on a camp stove, and we used small heaters to keep us warm. As I recall, it wasn't all that bad; we were a family and the children all got along so well.

When the ice storm was over we returned to my place on the hill. Bob was there with me, and we found that the water pipes had frozen and broken and that my plants were all dead. The water in the toilet was frozen and the toilet had cracked. Even the water in my coffee pot was frozen. I sat down in the kitchen and cried. Bob was there to console me and said he would make arrangements to get it all taken care of. What a sweet man! Someone was finally caring about me.

That night as we were having supper at Bob's house, Bob asked the children if they would all like to live together. I was astounded. The children all cheered and said yes. Bob looked at me and asked, "What about it? Would you like to move in with me and the boys?" I was really happy that he had made the decision a family one and again cried. Only this time they were tears of joy.

Trying to maintain two households, going to school, and moving the children from my house to Bob's house every few days had been taking a toll on me.

We did everything as a family, and I was very happy. I really cared about Bob and the boys and it just seemed so right that we were all together like this. This was the type of family life I had always wanted for the children, and now we finally had it.

In 1977, Bob and I got engaged. We started making plans to remodel the house to make more room for all of us. At that time no wedding date was set because we wanted to make certain the house was done and that I had graduated and had a good-paying job. After all, it was quite expensive to support nine of us, and I certainly didn't expect Bob to take on that kind of responsibility without my help. We converted the original attached garage into a master bedroom. We added another bathroom where a closet had been and started building a new large unattached garage next to the house.

We continued to do everything as a family. The seven children were very close and were quite protective of each other. I felt good knowing that and hoped they would always be as close as brothers and sisters.

When we were ready to paint the house, Bob and I chose several shades of blue. Then we all had a vote to choose which color it would be. We all agreed on blue-ribbon blue. What the paint store folks failed to mention was that we should have used a color that was at least one or two shades lighter than the paint card that we chose because the actual color is usually brighter than the card. However, we chose our color, bought the paint, and started painting the house only to discover that it was really a bright blue. The kids liked it, but Bob and I had our reservations. It was too late now, the painting had begun and there was no turning back. It was a big job, but we all helped and got the job done.

That summer we planted a huge garden in the backyard. The children had to help. We had potatoes, corn, tomatoes, cucumbers—if we could name it, we had it. I had a huge job of making tomato juice and canning pickles. It was a labor of love for me, and the entire family appreciated it.

In the fall I began classes again full-time. I also started working part-time at Kohler Company, a local plumbingware manufacturing company, through the co-op program at school. It seemed like an extra strain on me, but I knew it was a good experience and hoped, perhaps, I could get a job there after I graduated. The children all helped out, and we were managing quite well. We all seemed happy.

That year we had another ice storm. It was not as bad as the last one, but again the power was off for several days. When the power came back on we looked around to see if anything was damaged. The basement had flooded from the sump pump not working, and all my furniture was ruined. Almost everything I had left was under water or water stained. I was able to salvage a few items of Larry's that I had saved for the children such as the letter sweater and the guestbook from the funeral. Most of the other stuff was water logged or covered with mold or mildew and had to be thrown out.

Some of Bob's stuff was ruined, too, but we were not going to let this get us down. We just cleaned it up, got rid of what we had to, and moved on. Kind of ironic that the things I worked so hard to save from Ken's clutches ended up being destroyed after all. But an act of nature was better than an act of jealousy, rage, and pure meanness.

At Christmas, Bob and I started talking more seriously about our wedding. We were going to make it fun. All seven children would be in the bridal party, and it would truly be a grand event. We knew we would not be allowed to marry in the Catholic Church because we had both been divorced, but that wasn't going to stop us. I pictured the dream wedding I would finally have. I pictured the boys in tuxedos and the girls all in cute flowing gowns of different colors. And the best part was we were uniting as a family. I was so happy. I finally was truly happy. I had everything I ever wanted, a happy family life, a handsome man, a nice house, a good education, and a bright future. I even had lots of dreams of happily ever after—a real Cinderella ending! And most importantly the children were all happy, too. Everything seemed right in our lives.

18
A Real Test of Faith

May 3, 1978, seemed like a normal day. I got the children off to school. Bob was on the road, and I had classes to attend. Around nine o'clock a strange feeling came over me. As I stood and looked out the kitchen window, I decided I should stay home from classes that day.

At about eleven o'clock, the telephone rang. It was Bob. He was at a restaurant on the highway about a half-mile from our house. He had the rig and was on his way for a delivery. I asked him if he wanted me to join him for lunch. He said no, he didn't have time, but he asked what I was doing that day. I said I wasn't going to school but that I had to get some groceries. Bob said I shouldn't leave the house. I asked him why, but he said he didn't know, just don't leave. I said I would do as he asked but kind of shrugged my shoulders. He said he loved me and I said I loved him too and we hung up.

At approximately eleven-thirty the telephone rang again. It was a good friend of Bob's whom he worked with. He said he had bad news and he wanted me to hear it from him instead of on the radio. Bob had been traveling around a curve near Kiel when he lost control of the rig. They believed the load must have shifted throwing the rig off balance. The tractor and trailer had rolled over. Bob was dead.

I remember falling to the floor and crying. *Dear God why are you doing this to me?* I asked. *I finally find true happiness and you yank it from me. Why? What about the children? Todd and Terry will never understand this. First their mother leaves them and now their father leaves them, too?* My mind was racing in one hundred directions. *What am I supposed to do, God? How can I continue?*

Bob had asked me to stay home but didn't know why. Had God been trying to tell him he was going to die, but Bob didn't understand it in those words? I had also had a premonition that something was not right. I knew something was going to happen, but I didn't know what. Are we warned in advance in some way about these things, but never truly understand that is what's happening? It sure appeared that way.

I telephoned my mom and dad, and they said they would be right over. I just sat slumped in a chair in disbelief. I was numb with pain and heartache. I don't remember in what order people started arriving at the house. Someone from the school had told Todd and Terry to go home because they were needed there. Todd and Terry rode their bicycles home from school. They came in the door and saw me crying. They knew something had happened to their dad. I had to tell them he was gone. It was unbearably painful. We all hugged and cried together. It seemed like the house was full of people. Everyone was asking what he or she could do. All I could think of was bring Bob back to us.

One of our neighbors was the principal of the local high school. He telephoned the pharmacy and somehow ordered a hundred Valium pills for me. I don't remember if I was asked who my doctor was and what pharmacy I went to. All I know is that all of a sudden I had all these pills that I was petrified of. This was the very pill I had almost taken my life with, and I surely wasn't going to take them now. I decided I would get through this with God's help. He was the only one that could help me now. How could they have gotten so many Valium without a doctor? I figured I would place them out of sight and get rid of them when this was all over.

Someone telephoned Lakeshore Technical College for me and explained that I would not be returning to class for a while. These were the final weeks of school with all the exams. I was terrified that I would not graduate now. They also telephoned Kohler Company because I was still working there part-time.

For the next few days, the children and I were never left alone, and Bob's family immediately took charge of everything. I was so grateful for that. They were always kind people. I guess they saw I was in no condition to do anything.

Tom McCue came to see me. We walked outside to get away from the commotion of the house. I know it was hard for him to talk to me since we were both crying. He said, "Life doesn't come with guarantees for happiness. You just have to take it where you can get it and enjoy what you have. Be glad you had such good times as a family with Bob. Be proud of how far you had come since Ken left. Some day you will be happy again."

It was comforting to have him near; he was such a dear friend. But I wasn't sure what happy was any more. Every time I was happy, it was ripped out from under me. All I ever wanted was peace, love, and happiness. Was that such a hard thing to ask for? Was I ever going to have peace in my heart? Was surviving life the only thing in my life?

The family asked if there was anything special I would like done. The only thing I could think of was to place the wedding ring on his finger. We had bought matching rings for our wedding. They honored my wishes, and everyone was so kind at the funeral. I was treated as Bob's wife. It was all so very painful.

At the cemetery, the children and I each took a carnation off the casket. I took a pink one; Todd and Terry took blue ones; and the other children each took a different color. When we returned to Bob's parent's home after the funeral, we put the flowers in a vase in the kitchen.

Over the next few days, Bob's family helped with all the cards and thank-you notes. There were so many. He was loved by so many. Why did someone so special have to die so young? The children and I had stayed at his parent's house through all of this, but now it was time to return home.

I was thirty-seven years old and, once again, was returning home to an empty house. I had seven children, but the house was empty without Bob there with us. *What now?* I wondered. We had only been together as a couple for a short while and never got to enjoy the uniting of our families. Did Bob have us protected as he had once told me? Did he actually make provisions for us? I was hoping they would let Todd and Terry stay with us. After all, I had been their mom for four years now. Fear set in. I had so many responsibilities now. How was I going to manage this heavy burden?

My thoughts went to the Valium I had put away. No, I was not going to fall into that trap. I had a future, even though I wasn't sure what kind. I had to think about the children. When the children were asleep I took the bottle of pills and flushed them down the toilet. I was relieved that they were gone and I could no longer even consider them.

The following weekend we returned to Bob's parent's home for Sunday dinner. I was very surprised to see that the only carnations still going strong were the two blue ones and the pink one. I wanted to believe it was because Bob wanted us to know he was with us.

The family had bought gifts for the children whose birthdays were close; Laura, Todd, Terry, and Michael had all been May babies. It was nice that they were so thoughtful, but it wasn't the same without Bob.

At the family gathering I was asked if I had gotten a lawyer. I said no I didn't think I needed one. They advised me to do so. This was going to be a sticky situation.

Bob had not provided for me, and technically I was out on the street. I understood that things wouldn't automatically go to me because we were not married yet. However, Bob had said to me that he had taken steps to help me if anything would happen to him. I guess he never had time to do that. Even the furniture was not mine. My things had been ruined in the flood in the basement. The house belonged to Todd and Terry and would be sold to someone else unless I could buy it for fair market value. I had no money. I panicked. What was it they were trying to say by telling me to get a lawyer! They were taking the boys from me! No way, I would fight. Was this the side of the family I hadn't seen? I tried not to think like that because I knew they were concerned for the boys and rightfully so.

My life had to get back on track. I had school to finish and graduation and my job at Kohler Company.

I went back to school and the instructors all helped me get through the exams. Despite enduring another life catastrophe, I had managed to get an associate degree in Materials Management. In June of 1978, I walked across the stage at Lakeshore Technical College and received a diploma. I heard seven children yell out, "Way to go Mom." My mom, sister, brother, and sister-in-law were also there to support me. Tears welled up in my eyes, and I knew that Bob and Larry were there with us, too. I had made it.

Kohler Company offered me a permanent position in the plumbingware scheduling office. I was a full-time employee. My perseverance had paid off. I had gotten myself out of the bar scene and received a degree. My children were proud of me. This was supposed to be the beginning of a bright and happy future. But my future was uncertain; I had a lot of unfinished business ahead of me. I guess it just didn't seem all that great without a partner to share it with.

Later that same June, I retained a lawyer so that I could go to court for custody of Todd and Terry. My lawyer told me I did not have a good chance because I had five other children and my future was not stable. I didn't care. I couldn't let Todd and Terry have another mother walk away from them, and I would do whatever it took to make the courts know I loved them and wanted them with me.

There were three families trying to get guardianship: Bob's sister Mary and her husband Jack; Joan's brother Jim and his wife Laura; and me.

Todd and Terry talked to the judge, but they were technically not old enough to decide for themselves where they wanted to be.

The court decided Todd and Terry should go live with Bob's sister Mary and her husband Jack. They had three boys of their own and were very good parents. I guess if I couldn't have them, Jack and Mary would have been my choice as well. I knew Todd and Terry would have the best care with them. Jack and Mary were the type of parents who were involved with their sons in all kinds of sports and who were very family oriented.

I asked that I be the one to tell them, since all seven children were waiting together in the hall outside the courtroom. I tried not to cry. It was a hard thing to do, and my heart felt like it had been ripped out once more. The children all cried because it seemed so unfair. I was numb and just felt like life was cruel. Where was my life going now—what else was I to lose?

Jack and Mary never said when they would come to get the boys. I knew they had to go and that it would be soon. I thought the best thing I could do now is try to make the best of it and keep things as normal as possible until that day arrived.

During the summer months, beginning the weekend of Memorial Day, the local townships had firemen's picnics. It was a chance for the children to go on rides, play games, and just have fun. Was I being disrespectful by doing this so soon after Bob's death? We were never married so I wasn't a widow again. But it was basically the same thing. I wasn't even thinking rationally any more. Life was short, that's all I knew, and I was going to make the children as happy as I could while I had them all together. I didn't even care what other people thought. *Let them walk a mile in my shoes and see if they can even survive*, I thought.

At one of the picnics I met Charlie Grueschow. I had met him before but was not sure where I had met him. He was very tall, six foot three, and weighed about 225 pounds. He asked me to dance, and I accepted. He was so kind and gentle for being so big. Charlie asked for my phone number, and I gave it to him.

Every night Charlie would call to see how we were all doing. He heard the whole story about Larry, Ken, and now Bob. Charlie was so sympathetic about all the things I had gone through. He said he wished he could take all the pain away.

I liked talking to him; he made me feel safe. He asked me out, and I went. I knew I was not ready to have a relationship, but what the heck, it was a shoulder to lean on.

I received a call from Jack and Mary. The time had come for the boys to get moved in with them and get settled before school started. They requested we make this as painless as possible and asked that I not call them or come over. It was to be a transition period during which they felt the boys would be better off not bringing up the past. I represented the past and the pain and, therefore, was refused visitation or telephone calls. I understood what they were trying to do and respected their wishes, but I don't believe they had any idea what they were actually asking me to do. Two of my children were leaving the family. The family wouldn't be the same, not ever. Would Todd and Terry think I had walked away from them, too? I wasn't given a choice; I had to respect their wishes.

The boys took their clothes and all the things they wanted. We all tried to think of it as a temporary thing, that they were merely going to visit. It was very difficult helping them pack.

I knew it was just a matter of time now before I would be told to leave the house. While Bob and I were living together we shared expenses. We figured out the bills and grocery allowance for the month and split it down the middle. I would write a check out to Bob who paid the bills from his checking account. I had saved all those checks. When I presented them to Jim (Joan's brother) who was executor of the estate, he told me I would receive some sort of repayment. Bob never paid me for babysitting while he was out of town, so I didn't feel bad about asking for something. I had to have help, and if this is what I had to do, oh well! I almost felt like I was stealing from the boys because, after all, everything belonged to them now. I consoled myself by thinking Bob would have wanted me to have something. Jim told me I could stay at the house until I found another place to move to.

19
My Best Friend Returns

I don't know what month it was, but I received a telephone call from Mary. She told me Joan was back in Wisconsin and staying with her brother and his family. Mary told me that Joan was going to try to claim the house and insurance money and fight for custody of the boys. My response to that was over my dead body. I told Mary I would help them in any way I could.

I was so upset because all I could hear in my head was Ken saying he wanted the insurance money and monthly income from social security. It sounded like the very thing he would go for. It was not going to happen; I would fight with all my might to prevent it. How dare they return and try to take everything after all the pain they had inflicted on our children and families! No, I was going to stop it no matter what it took.

I decided I would go see Joan at her brother's house, so I called and made an appointment to visit. I am sure Joan was nervous because she had no idea how I was going to react.

When I arrived, Ken was nowhere in sight, but I suspected he was around the corner or upstairs listening to our conversation. Joan told me social security had found her and told her about Bob's death. She said Ken had told her to come back and get her sons. Right! That's not what Ken wanted; he saw dollar signs. He had no scruples and would hover like a vulture. Apparently, she fell hard for his mind games, too. This was an act of kindness in her eyes not the vicious money-grubbing man that I knew. This man had such a power over women.

Joan was very surprised that Bob and I weren't already married. I told her Bob and I tried to heal from the hurt before we ever even thought about each other. I had helped him survive, and he helped me survive. There was nothing going on between us when she and Ken had left. We had only been engaged a short time before Bob died.

Joan had a very surprised look on her face. I realized Ken must have convinced her that Bob and I had a relationship from the beginning, from even before they left. I could read it in her face.

I told her outright I was going to try to prevent her from getting anything, even the boys. Joan asked why I was being so hard on her! I was almost speechless. How could she ever ask that, after what they had done? I spent four years of my life trying to rebuild a family foundation after they had left, and now that was all gone, too.

I said, "You ran off with my husband when we needed him most. Michael sent me out to that parking lot three times to look for his dad. You took care that your boys would be safe at a babysitter, but you left my four children alone all night. Alone! That was child endangerment." She commented that Ken had said Diana often babysat the kids and they would be fine by themselves. I told her we had never left them alone all night and that they had been scared. At that point I could tell I was shaking and getting so upset that I couldn't talk anymore. I told her I had to leave, and I left.

While driving home I was in tears. I thought, *I could kill her, plead momentary insanity, and get away with it*. After all I had been through I didn't think any jury would convict me. But as angry as I was, I knew I couldn't go that far. I could never kill anyone, but I could and I would fight with all my might to keep them away from all of it, and God would help me.

When the actual court date arrived I heard that Joan had changed her mind and only wanted to claim custody of her children. Sorry, but I couldn't allow that either because Ken was not a good dad and the boys would be abused. Ken was not in the courtroom with her. What a coward!

When it was my turn on the witness stand her lawyer tried to make it look like Bob and I were having an affair from the beginning. I was asked about the night Bob spent in my bed. I told the lawyer what had happened. I explained that I had gone to bed first because I was very tired and when I woke up Bob was in my bed but was on top the covers and was fully clothed. I was very embarrassed that it had happened, and we were not having an affair.

Joan again had that look of total shock like Ken had convinced her it was true. I knew Ken was a con man, and I was sure by now she knew it, too.

It came out in court that Joan had had an abortion during her time with Ken. Being Catholic, this was against her religion. Again I knew that must have been at Ken's request and that she had done what he asked; whereas, I had not. *He has put her through hell already*, I thought.

It was also brought out in court by a close friend of Joan's, Pat Karnitz, that Joan had had an affair during her marriage to Bob. Things were not looking good for Joan.

Mary and Jack's lawyer wanted to know how Joan could go four years without calling her children or even sending gifts or cards to them for their birthdays. She had made no contact whatsoever. It certainly looked as though she hadn't cared about their success in school or even their general health, and yet now she was claiming she wanted them back?

Joan also claimed she did not know Ken was married before or that he had a little boy. That was a bold-faced lie because I had told her that day when we picked up my car before they left together.

Joan lost her case for custody, and the boys remained with Jack and Mary. We had won, and Joan and Ken had lost. Ken only lost the insurance money he was after and the monthly income from social security that he could have lived on. Joan had lost her children and her credibility. She was declared an unfit mother. How low can you go!

Well, at least I didn't have to shoot her, I thought. Now, I could continue on knowing that she was defeated and that Bob could rest in peace. I thanked God again for helping me through that.

20
Another Betrayal

Charlie continued to call. It was so nice having someone there for me who was big, strong, and understanding. We dated and had fun together. He was like a knight in shining armor to me.

In August he asked me to go out for a special dinner. I wasn't sure what special was supposed to mean, but I said yes I would go. Charlie had it all planned. He said, "I have loved you from the moment we danced at the picnic, and I want to protect you from all the hurt and cruelty in life. Will you marry me?" He told me to think about it for a few days and he would ask me again really soon. I was shocked, yet not too much in life surprised me any more. I was not ready to get married, but the thought of being alone after all I had gone through and would still have to go through, was really scary. I honestly believe I wasn't able to make a rational decision. I was grabbing at whatever happiness I could get. I never knew what was coming next. I had no feelings, and I didn't care. I wasn't in any condition to make life-altering decisions, but I told him I would think about it. I remembered what Tom McCue had said that life does not come with guarantees and that you have to take happiness whenever you can. It had only been three months since Bob's death, and I was still empty from that. What was happiness anyway?

When Charlie asked me again, I said yes, I would marry him. He was like a gentle giant who was taking on a huge responsibility. I had five children, and I had to move again. He wanted to be there for all of us. What a hero!

Charlie found a new unfinished house that he loved on Aurora Road in a subdivision outside of Plymouth. We discussed the down payment and where we would get the loan. I hadn't received the money from the estate yet, since sometimes that can take a long time. I asked if he could get a veteran's loan because the interest rates were lower. Charlie said he asked and they said he didn't qualify. Charlie suggested we ask the seller if they could take a minimum down payment of a few hundred dollars until we got the money from the estate. They agreed, and it was a deal.

We would have a new house to move into as soon as we picked out the paint colors, fixtures, and flooring.

My oldest son, Leary, who was fifteen, was against my marrying Charlie. He came to me defiantly and said if I married Charlie he was going to run away. Leary had no specific reason; he just didn't want to have another dad. I told Leary he was not going to control my life and I would not allow him to blackmail me into giving up whatever chance I had for happiness. I told Leary life was short and asked him when all the kids were grown up and out of the house, what would there be for me! Did he want me to be alone all my life because he didn't like Charlie? Leary said no, of course not, he wanted me to be happy. The other children didn't talk to me about it. Charlie was good with the children, but I was going to make certain they would never be abused again. I even went so far as to warn Charlie that if he ever hurt me or the children he was gone.

Charlie liked the stock car races, and we went every Saturday night. It was a ritual with him. Saturday was race night and nothing else should be going on. I met a lot of his friends and they appeared to be good people. There was a little too much beer drinking, but no one was forcing me to drink it.

In September of 1978, we moved into the new house on Aurora Road in Plymouth. The children didn't have to change schools so that was a blessing. It was a really nice neighborhood, and we had a beautiful house. It was in the country about three miles out of town, so the children would have to ride the school bus. I also didn't have to worry about them hanging around on the streets because unless they found a way to town they stayed home.

Charlie and I started planning our wedding. It would be very simple. It would not be a fancy church wedding because that dream of mine had died. We did not want anyone to know that we were planning to get married, so we sent out invitations announcing a double birthday party. Charlie's birthday was in September, and mine was October. The children and our families knew about the wedding, but no one else did.

On September 30, 1978, I married Charlie at the justice of the peace's home in Sheboygan. We went directly to the party and announced that we had gotten married. It was a huge surprise that everyone seemed to be happy about. Actually I didn't care if they weren't happy because it was done, and I was heading into a new life.

Diana was seventeen; Leary was fifteen; Michael was twelve; Cindy was ten; and Laura was seven. It certainly was a full house.

My daughter Diana was dating. She was in an on-again-off-again relationship with Tony Gahagan. Tony was very nice and good-looking, but like any other young man he liked to have fun. Too often, it seemed, he was with his buddies while she stayed home. She got pregnant in December of 1978 while she was a senior in high school. I was not happy about it, but nothing in life shocked me or surprised me anymore.

The times had changed since my youth. She was not banned from school for being pregnant, and she would be allowed to graduate with her class in June of 1979. I was proud that she was able to get her diploma and had not totally ruined her life.

My first grandchild was born August 16, 1979. They named her Amanda. She was a beautiful child, and I know Diana and Tony both loved her.

About that time, I had changed positions within Kohler Company and was working in the stockroom of the whirlpool area. I liked the idea of wearing blue jeans to work and not having to keep up with the fashions in the office. I couldn't afford all the new clothes and shoes the other women in the office wore.

Then, much to my dismay, I found out that my foreman was taking classes at Lakeshore Technical College for the same degree I already had. *What was wrong with that picture*, I thought! I was working for someone who did not even have the education that I had and he was my boss. I spoke to my foreman, and he recommended I go to the personnel department and update my file to include my degree, which I did. I took a few tests and in January of 1980 was promoted to foreman in the brass building at the Kohler Company.

I recall Charlie teasing me that I wouldn't make a good boss. Of course the don't-tell-me-I-can't-do-something attitude kicked in, and I had to prove him wrong.

One night Diana, who was then nineteen, and I met at a local bar. We had a good relationship, and I enjoyed her adult company. We were not only mother and daughter, but also friends. She had her own apartment now, and seemed so grown up living her own life.

Diana and I were talking about everything that had happened in our lives and that was when she told me Ken had molested her as a child. I was horrified and asked why she hadn't told me. Diana said she hadn't told me because I had been through so much already she only wanted me to be happy. She said it was too frightening and painful for her to talk about as a child but now, as an adult, she was able to admit it happened. I felt so bad for her. I had no idea and wished I could have made the pain go away. She said she was OK now but her hate for Ken would never go away. She said that when Ken left she was secretly celebrating. She was relieved.

It seemed like everyday life was uneventful for a while, until October 15, 1981, when my dad died. Mom telephoned me, and this time it was my turn to be with her while she was in pain. I went to tell Charlie what had happened and where I would be. As I recall he never offered to go with me.

I was devastated. Bob's death was still fresh in my mind, and it was very painful. I loved my dad very much. I had a hard time helping Mom pick out a casket for Dad, and my brother and sister ended up making most of the decisions. *Why do people we love have to die! I know that is what the cycle of life is all about, but it is always so terribly painful.* With God's help we managed to get through it.

As life would have it, just a few short days later, on the evening of October 24, 1981, Tony was killed in a car accident. We were told he was with several friends when the car went off the road. Tony got out to go get help, walked into some downed electrical wires, and was electrocuted.

Would the pain never end! Tony was only twenty-three years old, and his and Diana's daughter was just two years old. What tragedy! Diana was heartbroken. They had just gotten back together as a couple and had hoped to make a go of it for Amanda's sake. But it wasn't meant to be.

Diana was sobbing heavily, and Charlie was trying his best to comfort her. I remember thinking that she was just twenty years old and was already petrified that her life was going to parallel mine. She was wondering how she would manage to raise Amanda all by herself. I felt awful that I couldn't answer her because I knew what my life had been like so far and prayed her life would be different. Life surely could be cruel and harsh. The only advice I had for her was to be strong for Amanda's sake and eventually the pain would go away.

I made a huge career change in April of 1984 and became a security guard at the Kohler Company. I knew if I left supervision it might be a long time before I could get back into it, but I had to take that chance. I was no longer happy in the brass building. The general supervisor and I had been clashing and four years of that was enough.

Michael had graduated from high school and decided to go west to live in Arizona. He was the adventurous type so I was certain he would be fine. We only had Cindy and Laura at home now.

It seemed that around that time my daughter Cindy started acting up. She was sixteen and a normal teenager. Cindy was dating a young farmer named David. She was moody, got into trouble, and was totally rebelling against me. Her grades went down, and she was gone a lot with her friends. I couldn't talk to her at all; she had closed the door completely to our mother-daughter relationship. *Many times I cried and wondered if I was such a good mother after all. What had I done? Why couldn't I get through to her?*

On Christmas Eve of 1984, Cindy and David Oberrich announced their engagement. They never consulted any family members, just became engaged. I was not happy because she was too young, only sixteen. However, there was no talking them out of it. I realized I couldn't change it and had to accept the fact that she was going to marry him with or without my blessing.

Then a few months later, Cindy came home with David by her side and told us she was pregnant. My first instinct was to get angry, but where would that have gotten me? Cindy was so young, only a junior in high school. She said she was going to drop out of school and marry David. I tried to convince her she should finish school first, but she said no she was just quitting. I realized that nothing I could say would change her mind. After that she spent most of her days at David's house. I made up my mind that as a parent I had done the best that I could and it was time to let go.

One day, Cindy and David had come to our house for some reason, I guess to pick up some of her clothes. Cindy was very rude and short with me. I was hurt when she said she didn't want me as her friend, that she had enough friends, and that she didn't care if I had that type of relationship with Diana and Laura. I remember asking her why she was so mean to me. What had I done to cause this hatefulness? Charlie was standing at the other end of the kitchen, and she shouted out that I should ask him because he had molested her. I froze! What? My stomach was churning. Charlie immediately asked to speak to Cindy in the living room alone, and she agreed. David was standing at the door, and I was at the table thinking my knees were going to give out and I would fall to the floor. I felt nauseous. When Cindy came out into the kitchen, I said I thought it best that they just leave now and we would speak again soon.

I don't remember much about the conversation I had with Charlie after that. I know I was sobbing uncontrollably. He tried to convince me he had been drunk, had told Cindy he was sorry, and had tried to make it up to her. He pleaded with me not to dump all our years of marriage on a mistake that he regretted and had apologized for. He couldn't take it back but would if he could. Cindy was now getting married and moving on. It was in the past and couldn't we just get past this. I stared out the window. I couldn't speak to him; I was frozen.

I think back now and wish I had asked him to leave, but I didn't. I don't know why. Perhaps I just wanted it to all go away. The man who was going to protect us all had turned into the enemy. I remember thinking *where else will my life go wrong?*

One day within the next few weeks, Cindy came to me and told me she had kept things a secret because she did not want to be the one to rip our family apart again. She said she did not want to be the one to make us lose our home and have to start over again. So much pain, yet she tried to protect me from being unhappy. I did not know what to say to her that she would go to that length to keep her family in tact.

Is this a pattern? Have all my children suffered in secret to protect me? Are there more secrets out there? Lord I hope not, I told myself.

So that was why she was always in trouble and couldn't get close to me. It was because she was afraid she would tell me, and she just simply thought it best to stay away as much as she could.

I loved my daughter with all my heart and to see that she finally got this terrible secret off her chest was amazing. We had finally torn down the wall that was between us. It would not be forgotten, but we could move on.

I often wondered what they would think if I told them I had been molested, too, as a teenager by an uncle and a cousin. I had also kept quiet because I did not want to shame the families. How disgusting! Two of my daughters had to experience the same shameful event that I had.

That should have been the end of my marriage right then, no questions asked, just over with. But I was desperate to make my marriage work. After everything I had already been through, I did not want to start over. As painful as that was I just wanted to hang on. I did not want to destroy my life again. I know my relationship with Charlie was one string short of broken, but we both promised to try.

In February of 1985 I was promoted to supervisor–security at the Kohler Company. That should have been a happy time for me, but other things were going on that took away the joy of a promotion.

On August 4, 1985, Cindy and David were married. I wasn't involved with the wedding as much as I should have been. Maybe I thought it best not to be too close because it would remind Cindy of what had happened. It was a nice wedding, and she appeared to be happy. I prayed that my daughter had found true love and would be happily married forever.

On February 2, 1986, Cindy delivered a healthy baby girl, and they named her Chelsie. She was adorable and my daughter seemed truly happy to have a daughter of her own.

Diana had married a motorcycle-riding party guy named Rusty. I was worried about her because I knew it wouldn't last. I was right; they soon divorced.

Then Diana dated and married Michael Born. He was a truck driver, at the time, for a local sand and gravel company. Michael was very tall and nice looking. He had been a friend of Tony Gahagan. He was a good husband and provider.

She became pregnant and had a very hard time with the pregnancy and the delivery. On April 16, 1987, Diana delivered a baby boy. They named him Michael after his dad. The marriage was not meant to be; after several years they divorced as well.

Leary was dating a lovely girl named Brenda who had a little girl of her own named Crystal. They seemed like they were happy. Brenda became pregnant, and on September 7, 1988, they had a little girl. They named her Tequila. I thought that was a strange name, but it was not my decision. She was an adorable little girl.

21
The Final Straw

Charlie became increasingly annoyed with his job. I wanted to help him and suggested he go to school and take some classes. After all, I had done well taking classes at Lakeshore Technical College. Charlie said no, he was not going back to school. I knew he liked making furniture, and he was good at it, but he was never satisfied with his work. He had made me a rolltop desk that turned out beautifully. He had also made some end tables and a sewing table for me. I told him he should pursue that as a career and start his own business. No he didn't want to do that either.

I then asked Charlie what it was that he wanted. What would make him happy! Charlie confided in me that he had always dreamed about owning his own dump truck and starting his own business making deliveries of sand and gravel. I suggested we research that idea and see if we could buy a truck for him.

We talked to the bank and bought a dump truck. Charlie's dream was moving in the right direction. He had it painted a metallic blue, and he was so proud of it. Proud was nice, but we needed a paycheck. Charlie started putting bids on jobs and making deliveries. But when he got home at night, he had to clean the truck, make repairs, and do the paperwork. It became overwhelming for him. I guess he finally realized that going to a job in the morning and punching out at the end of the day wasn't so bad after all. He could go home and relax, rather than work some more. He kept plugging away at it, though, hoping to make it a decent business. Then we got word that the government was making legal changes that would require the little guy with one truck to charge more than a business that had a fleet, and Charlie could no longer be competitive. We had to sell the truck, and Charlie needed to find another job.

Charlie was offered a position as operations manager at a local sand and gravel company. That was a good position. I knew Charlie was good at figuring sand and gravel, but he had no training in supervising employees. That job was short-lived, and he went back to driving a truck and hauling milk for a local cheese company.

In July of 1989, Leary was planning his wedding. The wedding date fell on the same day as my thirtieth high school reunion, July 15, 1989. That was a shame because I had wanted to go, but my son was far more important. Charlie said I should do both and leave Leary's wedding reception to go to the class reunion. I hoped he was only kidding, this was my son we were talking about and I was not going to do any such thing. So much for Charlie's family values!

Leary's bachelor party was the Saturday before the wedding. Charlie was already grumbling because it was on a Saturday night and we weren't supposed to do anything but go to the stock car races on Saturday nights. I told him he was going to the party and could go to the races later that night when the party ended. Charlie took me to the races and then he left to go to the party. I would see him later.

Later came sooner than I thought. Charlie said he couldn't find the address of the party and was not going to ride around all night looking for the place. I was livid. He hurt my son because he couldn't give up the stupid stock car races! I did not believe his excuse.

Over the next year, my disgust and contempt for him was growing every day. Charlie and I had many disagreements, and our marriage was on the rocks, for sure. We didn't seem to have anything in common any more. He was selfish and childish, and we were in two different worlds.

He was jealous of my job that I got paid days off and paid vacation. I made more money than he did, and that didn't sit well with him either.

He began to hoard the money from his paycheck. At one point he claimed that I was spending too much and I shouldn't even need his money to pay the bills. I was so fed up, I threw the checkbook at him and said fine then you take care of it, you pay the bills. I told him I would sign my checks over to him, and he would have to deal with it. The bills piled up unopened and laid on the desk for weeks. I couldn't deal with that, so I cleaned it up and no more was said about money.

Charlie seemed so childish at times, but by now maybe I was looking for things to annoy me. I didn't need another child; I needed a husband who would stand by me through thick and thin. I no longer had the big protector, but rather a selfish child. He had even gone so far as to hide candy and cookies in a cabinet he called his own.

Diana dated and married Eric Juhlin. She truly seemed in love, and I prayed that he would be the one to really make her happy. She had been through so much, and I often wondered if she was having trouble finding happiness because of the life I had when she was growing up. If I had done this to my daughter, I was truly sorry. I never meant to hurt any of my children.

In February of 1991, my mom became ill. She was having heart problems. Mom needed to go to Milwaukee to have some tests run at a particular hospital that specialized in heart-related problems. My sister and I took her there and then came home because she had to stay overnight.

The following Sunday there was a snowstorm. I was restless and upset and worried about Mom. I wanted to go see her and make sure she was OK. Charlie told me the roads were too bad and my car was too unreliable in the snow, and he advised against it.

I was standing at the patio door, looking out into the backyard, and thinking about Mom when Charlie came in from the garage and said that he was driving to Milwaukee in his truck to go to a woodworking show.

I stood there in disbelief. Was I hearing him correctly? Had he just stated that he was going to Milwaukee for a woodworker's show and with no mention of my mom? He didn't offer to drive me to see her. He was thinking only of himself. *Is he that selfish?* I thought.

That was the final straw that would ultimately end my marriage. That was just too much. He had no sympathy or empathy, only his drive for self-gratification.

I packed a bag, took my chances with my car, and drove myself to Milwaukee to be with my mom. Not only did I need to go see her, but also I needed to get away from him.

When I was at the hospital that evening the doctor came in to speak to Mom. He told us Mom was on the list for a heart valve replacement. She would be going to surgery soon.

I prayed, thank you, Lord, for helping me to be with my mom before her surgery. I was the only one there for her. Had I not come, she would have been all by herself. How dreadful! I knew what that was like and didn't wish it on anyone.

I telephoned Charlie, my children, my sister, and my brother and told them Mom was headed for surgery.

The entire family showed up to wait with me for her to come out of surgery. The only conspicuously absent person was Charlie. It just showed how little he cared. I guess it made my decision that much easier, and I knew when I got home I would tell him I was filing for divorce.

I did just that. I told Charlie I couldn't live like that any more and didn't have to. As much as I wanted my marriage to turn out right, I just couldn't turn it around. It was time to end it. I was keeping the house because, after all, it was my money that made the down payment. Charlie didn't fight me on that and said he would move out.

I never gave myself a chance to heal from Bob's death before I moved on with Charlie and perhaps that made me even more at fault for that marriage not working out. It's not that I didn't love Charlie, because I did. It was because I never got Bob totally out of my heart and Charlie was not Bob.

Charlie moved into a trailer in the small town of Greenbush. I helped him by sorting out towels, dishes, pots and pans, and things like that. It was hard telling what he had already taken out of the house without my knowledge because I had to work, but I hadn't noticed anything major.

A few months later Charlie told me he had bought a house with a veteran's loan. What? I distinctly remembered having asked him to apply for a VA loan before we bought the house and him telling me that he didn't qualify. Charlie admitted he had never checked into it and just assumed he didn't qualify. I was so furious I started beating him on his chest with my fists. *How could he? Another marriage started in a lie.* How could he take all the money I had without even checking? Charlie had no answer and just said that he was sorry.

Our divorce was final on September 20, 1991. That marriage lasted for thirteen years. At least I had passed the seven-year mark, unlike my first two marriages.

I refinanced the house, bought some new furniture, and was very happy to be free. *Maybe now the stress level will come down and I can live a normal life,* I thought. But what was normal? I had never had a normal life for any considerable length of time. And for that matter, what was happiness! Everyone has her own ideas of what happiness is. I only wanted to be at peace with myself, be content and happy with what I had. Cinderella's idea of happily ever after did not apply to me.

By now my children had all left the house, too. Laura had an apartment of her own and was seriously dating Jim Wesenberg. He was a very good-looking blond guy who could have passed as a male model.

In October of 1991, Laura told me she was pregnant. She was twenty, had graduated from high school, and was making her own life. I was hoping more for her, though, than settling down with children. I always thought she would become a model because she had such a big, bright, beautiful smile. She had a cute figure and curly blond hair, too. But it was her life, and all I could do was to be there for support.

On July 20, 1992, Alexander James was born. My youngest daughter had a son. He was adorable, with blond hair just like his parents. I knew her life would never be the same, but I also knew she loved her son.

22
Good Samaritan

In the winter of 1991, three months after my divorce became final, just before Christmas I bumped into an old friend, Loretta Rizzi. She asked how I was doing, and I told her I was now divorced. She said her brother Jim Oberle had been looking for me for years and asked if I would please stop by to see him. I remembered Jim as a fun person whose wife Pat had been a dear friend. Loretta stated that Pat and Jim had divorced a couple of years ago and quite often Jim talked about finding me. She said he had a business in the basement of her tavern selling pictures and frames. I told her I would try to stop by soon.

I wanted to see Jim, but I did not wish to go alone. I asked my son Leary if he would go with me to see Jim's business. Leary went with me since he remembered Jim, too.

The visit was a surprise to Jim, but he seemed truly happy to see me. I bought some of the artwork for Christmas presents and told him I would be back. We exchanged telephone numbers.

For the next few months, we dated every once in a while. I noticed Jim seemed to drink a lot but was never totally drunk when he was with me. He seemed to be truly down about life itself. Although we never spoke about his divorce from Pat, I sensed he took it very hard.

I felt sorry for him because he and his son Jim Jr. were sharing an apartment that was cold and didn't have much furniture. It seemed like he was living in poverty.

Call it what you will, but I felt like a Good Samaritan when I offered for Jim and his son to come live with me. After all, I had a house with three bedrooms, and I was alone in it. They would pay me room and board, so the arrangement would also help me financially.

Jim and Jim Jr. moved in and all seemed fine for a few months. That was when I started finding empty bottles of alcohol in cabinets and in the basement. Someone was drinking pretty heavily, but it never occurred to me that Jim was a full-blown alcoholic. How could I have not seen that!

In the spring of 1992, a camping party was being planned for Memorial Day weekend. Some of our children, his and mine, were planning a camping holiday up north at Rock Dam. The plan was that Jim and I would join them but would not stay at the campsite. We planned a fishing trip and would stay at a motel in the area. The truth was that neither one of us wanted to sleep on the ground in a sleeping bag. I was really looking forward to the trip. It would be a mini vacation. I hadn't been fishing in years, and I was truly excited.

The area was beautiful, and it was so peaceful. *What a nice vacation,* I thought. We had a little bungalow-type room with two beds in it. It wasn't really fancy, but it sure beat the cold, hard ground. Jim and I had a nice dinner that night and went to bed at a reasonable time because we wanted to go fishing in the morning.

The next morning we went fishing, and it was so nice. I could have sat there all day listening to the bird's chirp and the water running down the river. I don't remember if we caught any fish or not. It didn't matter; it was so peaceful and restful.

That same afternoon we drove to where the children were camping. It was nice to see our children getting along and having fun together. We took some lawn chairs and sat and chatted with everyone.

I overheard a conversation Jim was having with one of his daughters. He told her he was finally going to have surgery on his knees and he was lucky to have someone who would take care of him.

I wondered when he was planning to spring this on me. I was no nurse, and I wasn't going to wait on him hand and foot while he recuperated. What nerve he had!

I had brought a six-pack of wine coolers for me to drink for the weekend, and Jim had brought a fifth of whiskey for himself. By evening Jim was out cold, he had consumed three-quarters of the bottle of whiskey. I wouldn't have just been out cold, I would have been dead had I drank that much.

The children were all going to the main building where there was going to be live music that night. They asked us to join them. Right! Jim couldn't even respond, so I said I would go and we could leave him there. It wasn't that far from the campsite, and I would leave him a note saying where I was. Why should I miss out on the fun because he was drunk?

I had a really nice time with the children. We laughed and danced the night away. About 11:00 PM, Jim came in the door and was in a really bad mood. I guess it was the hangover. He called me a witch for leaving him at the campsite. I just ignored him because I knew it was the alcohol talking. Instead of sobering up and having a soda or coffee, he started drinking mixed drinks like they were water.

When the music stopped it was time to go back to the motel, but I had no idea how to get back because I wasn't familiar with the area. Jim was calling me all kinds of foul names, and it was obvious to me he didn't care what I did. I told him he could either get in the car and help get us back to the motel or stay there and sleep on the ground in a tent. I guess at that point he knew how serious I was, and he got in the car.

All the way back to the motel we barely spoke a word, except to say which way to turn. When we got to our room I told Jim I was leaving in the morning. I told him our relationship was over and he would also have to find another place to live.

Jim became verbally abusive and called me several names again. He said I had ruined his vacation because I had had too many wine coolers. I told him he should look at his own bottle of whiskey that was almost empty.

I asked him when he was planning to tell me about his knee surgery, and he was surprised that I knew. He never answered me, so I suspect it was to be a surprise.

I was pleased with myself for standing my ground and sticking up for myself. It was my car and my house, and no one was going to treat me like that ever again. I had finally realized why I was finding empty bottles at home. He was an alcoholic, and he truly needed help.

It was a very quiet ride home. When we arrived I told Jim to leave his fishing gear in the garage because I meant what I had said, it was over and he was to move out.

When Jim Jr. arrived at home I told him what had happened and said I was sorry, but he had to move out along with his dad. He said he was also sorry, but he understood and would help look for another place to live.

In June of 1992 they moved out. Jim still owed me about four hundred dollars for rent, but I supposed I would never get that back.

I was relieved to be by myself again and vowed to stay that way. No more bad relationships I promised myself. I was done with men in general. What a nightmare my life had been! Why was I always hurting myself! I needed to heal for real this time. No more rebounds or sympathy for men. I needed to find me and make sure I was going to be all right. God help me! I truly needed guidance this time so I wouldn't continue to make bad choices.

My family received an invitation to Terry Lisowe's wedding. Terry was Bob's youngest son. It was set for June 12, 1993. Not only was it the same date that they had become engaged, but also it was Bob's birthday. How thoughtful that was!

We were all apprehensive about going to the wedding. We knew it would still be uncomfortable for us. But we would have to put that aside and be there for Terry.

When the day finally arrived I was very nervous. I was also very surprised when I was given a flower to wear like I was someone important. I was very moved by the gesture.

I saw Bob's family sitting up front in the wedding tent. My family and I sat behind Bob's family. I noticed Joan had come, but Ken was nowhere in sight.

She was also wearing a flower but was sitting in the back row. How appropriate I thought. This was payday for Joan. She should have been up front with her son and been a huge part of her youngest son's wedding, but instead she was in the back. I wondered how all this made her feel. It must have been very painful for her.

Surprisingly, I no longer held a grudge against her and only felt sympathy for her. She was paying dearly for her bad choices. I knew life could not have been easy for her. I also knew Ken was not fun twenty-four hours a day, and I was sure she had to learn that the hard way, very early in their relationship.

The wedding went well, and I was very proud of the handsome, intelligent, well-mannered person Terry had become. His wife, Ann, was beautiful and such a sweetheart. They seemed so happy together. I truly hoped nothing would ever make Terry sad again.

At the reception, it was very obvious the pain was still there. Bob's family sat in one section of the room. Joan's family sat in another section. And I was in the middle. Bob's family spoke with us and was very friendly, but Joan's family stayed away. I guess they weren't sure what I might say to them.

What they didn't know was that I truly wanted to speak to Joan and tell her I had forgiven her. I wanted to tell her it was time to forgive, let go, and move on. However, with all the tension in the room I knew this was not the right time.

That night at the reception, I had gone into the ladies room and was about to walk out, when a total stranger blocked the door. She said she was not letting me out until I told her who I was and why was I wearing a flower. I told her I was Bob's fiancée and had been Todd and Terry's mom for four years before Bob died. She said that explains the flower and how nice of them to do that. She walked out the door first and I stood in shock for a few seconds before walking out also. What nerve blocking the door!

When I walked back to our table I noticed the woman talking to a group of people. They all turned and looked at me at the same time. So much for trying to blend in with the crowd! Talk about uncomfortable! I found out later it was someone in the bride's family who wasn't sure who I was. We didn't stay long after that; it was too awkward.

In December of 1993, I was promoted to supervisor–security administration at the Kohler Company. I really liked my job and worked hard at making a difference. I believed you are only as good as the people working for you, and I did my best to convey that. I also tried not to give anyone an assignment that I would not have done myself. I truly liked the people I was working with.

My life finally seemed to be quiet, and I was at peace. I was OK without a mate. I didn't need someone in my life, and I felt free to be me. However, my life was about to take another huge turn.

23
Soul Mate

In June of 1994, my daughter Cindy had planned a birthday party at a local tavern. She was recently divorced from David, would be twenty-five years old, and just wanted to have some fun. She had set the date for Saturday, June 25.

Cindy asked me to join them for the celebration. David Klinzing, her friend, mentioned that his dad was widowed and wondered if she knew of any single women. Cindy told him her mom was single, and David said he would bring his dad to the party so we could meet. Cindy told me it would be nice if we met. The red flag came up, and I told her not to fix me up with anyone; I was not ready. But ready or not God had a new plan for me. A new road to take!

I remember praying on the way to the party. *God, please let it be someone who doesn't drink or smoke. Let it be someone who is kind and sincere. Am I asking too much? Is there actually someone out there like that?*

I remember the party like it was yesterday. I was having fun and dancing with my daughters. When the music ended I went to the bar and bought myself a wine cooler. Standing there looking out over the crowd, I saw a man in a black leather jacket who was watching the dancers. It was really strange because I remember I had tunnel vision directly to him. It was like no one else was in the room, and I remember thinking to myself, *God I hope it's him.*

I turned back to Cindy and her friends, when Cindy said she would like me to meet Roman Klinzing. It was Roman Klinzing Jr. and David Klinzing's father. This was the person they wanted me to meet. I turned around, and my heart skipped a beat. It was the man in the leather jacket.

We exchanged greetings and talked. I asked that he call me Geri, as that was what my friends called me. He offered to buy me a drink and said he didn't drink or smoke since quitting five years ago. I was awestruck. *Is this for real? It is what I just asked for*, I said to myself. We danced, and then he asked if I wanted to go talk outside because it was so loud in there. We went outside and found a ledge to sit on. The branches from the bush kept getting caught in my hair, and he politely broke the branch so it wouldn't bother me any more. How thoughtful.

He told me they had come on motorcycles, the ones parked by the door. I guess I shouldn't have been surprised since he was wearing a leather biker jacket.

He told me his wife had died a few months ago at the end of February and life did not seem worth living after that. He said he missed her very much and wished he could turn back the clock. I told him I understood and explained that I, too, had lost my husband and a fiancée and knew how painful it was. But I told him he would heal in time and life goes on.

He told me he had seven children, five girls and two boys, and he told me their names. I laughed and said I had a big family, too, that I had five children, three girls and two boys, and told him their names. We talked about our children and what they were all doing with their lives. We exchanged telephone numbers, and he said we should go out sometime soon. I told him I would like that, and we returned to the party.

I also met one of his daughters; her name was Patricia, and they called her Patti. Patti was a beautiful, blond girl who was very pleasant. She said they were having a baptism the next morning for her sister Brenda's son Cody. I told her I was glad to have met her and hoped they all had fun at their family gathering.

During the next few weeks, Roman and I saw each other often. He told me stories about having gone for a drive and wanting to run his car off a bridge to commit suicide because he missed his wife so much. It sounded so painful, and I knew God's plan was for me to help him through his uncontrollable grief. I could show him that you can overcome the pain of losing a loved one.

Apparently our relationship did not sit well with some of his family. Cindy told me that she saw Roman Jr. and David, Roman's sons, at a bar recently and David stood very close, in her face shouting and pointing his finger at her. He told her to tell her mother she should stay the hell away. Cindy said she stood firm and told him if he had something to say to her mother he should tell her himself, she wasn't his messenger.

It seemed truly odd since David was the one who wanted us to meet in the first place and now I was supposed to stay away.

I was not going to tolerate my daughter being approached and bullied about my relationship with Roman. So one day after work I drove out to their house to find David and confront him about his actions. Chris, Roman's grandson, and Roman Jr. were out in the workshop. Roman Jr. said that his dad was not home. I said I came out to see David because I understood he had something he wanted to say to me. He said David wasn't home either. I asked him to please tell David that I would be back.

As I drove away, I was wishing David had been home since I had mustered up all the courage I could find to go confront him and now would have to do it again. He now knew I was looking for him, and I couldn't and wouldn't back down.

The next night I went back. David was home, and I asked him to come out of the house so I could speak to him privately. He said yes he would come out. I told him I did not appreciate him approaching my daughter and if he had something to say to me he should tell me.

David said he was concerned for his father because his mother had died only a few months ago and his father was vulnerable. I told him I knew about his mother's death and that I was trying to help his father cope with her death. I told him he did not have to worry because I was only looking for companionship. I had no intentions other than that. I had my own car, a good-paying job, and a house of my own and didn't need these things from his father. I explained to him that I, too, had lost a husband and a fiancé and knew how painful it could be.

After we spoke David said he thought I would be all right for his dad and that we need not mention this to his father. I agreed. I wanted to tell Roman what a bully he had for a son, but I decided that if I wanted his son's trust I should keep quiet. I tried to understand how David might have thought it was his place to control and pick his father's friends. It was kind of ironic, since he was the one who wanted us to meet in the first place. I guess that should have been a warning as to what was ahead.

When I drove away I was relieved that I had followed through and had confronted David. At least he knew I wasn't going to let him intimidate me.

My life with Roman and his family is a book all by itself so I am not going to continue very deeply down that path. Perhaps I will write about it someday. All I can say is God wanted me to help Roman through the pain and suffering he experienced from the loss of his wife. It was what I was supposed to do! In the process I was at peace with myself and Roman, and it just seemed like we belonged together.

On November 8, 1994, there was a fire at Roman's place. The big workshop went up in flames, and he had no insurance on the building. When he came to me and told me about it, he was in tears. I tried to console him. He said he just didn't know how much more he could take. I assured him, this too would pass and it would all work out.

One day Roman told me he was considering selling his homestead. The workshop fire convinced him it was time to move on. He said he was in negotiations with Kohler Company to buy the property. The company wanted to build a golf course and his property was in the way.

In January of 1995, Roman made an agreement with the company for the purchase of his land. He had until December of 1995 to move. He said he had gotten a nice offer on it and that he had spoken to his children about it. They wanted him to save the house and move it onto another property.

We spent the next few weeks and months looking at property for him to move the house to. It seemed like the properties we found were just too far away to move a house. Looking for property seemed to consume all of our time.

Roman told me he had made an agreement with his oldest son David that he could have the house if he would pay back the moving expenses and all the expenses connected with the land and putting the house in place. Roman said David was really happy because he truly wanted the house and verbally made a gentleman's agreement on the deal.

It was about this time that Roman got a job working with a local log cabin building firm. He told me his wife had always wanted him to build a log cabin. He said she didn't want to live in it because she told him she never wanted to leave their homestead. But she knew it was what he liked to do. I was happy that he had a job he liked.

What he found out, though, was that he had to travel a lot and he did not like that part of the job. One job was in the hills of San Francisco, California. Roman said it rained almost every day and they didn't work on those days. He was bored just sitting around, and they didn't get paid for those days, either.

Roman and I spent all our free time together. We talked about moving in together. He stayed at my house a lot of the time.

Roman told me he was considering buying a house and then getting a loan on that property to get the homestead moved. That way everything would be separate, and the loan would only be used for the moving expenses. He asked me if I would consider selling my house and moving with him. I said I would.

At that time I recommended that Roman retire from his job and just get the work done that he needed to get done. Moving a house was not an easy task and would take much of his time. It just seemed the right thing to do. I had a good job, with a good income. We would be just fine. Roman agreed to do that.

In May of 1995, he put his plan into action. He found an unfinished log home in Two Rivers. It was a long ride for me to and from work every day, but it was a beautiful log house and it would be worth it. He thought it would be a good investment and the deal was made.

He also purchased land in Cleveland, in southern Manitowoc County, for the homestead to be moved to. It was a fifty-five-acre farm Roman had until the end of the year to get the house moved.

During that time, I sold my house and we moved in together in the log house he had purchased. Every day I drove forty-three miles to work and back, putting almost one hundred miles on my car each day. The days seemed long, and Roman was working very hard to get everything done.

Roman and I were happy together, but our children were from two different worlds. It was evident they would never be friends. They just didn't care much for each other. Roman's family was still having a hard time with the fact that I was in their father's life, and my children didn't like the way some of his children were treating me. All of my children showed respect to Roman and treated him with kindness. Some of his children treated me like I wasn't even there and some actually wished I wasn't.

It came out at a later date that some of his children were upset because they thought Roman had bought this big, beautiful log house for me and hadn't done that for their mother. They didn't think to talk to their dad about it; they just assumed. But, it was what she had wanted for him. Roman said she had made it very plain that she would never leave the homestead. She wanted him to have a log home someday because she knew it was his dream. In fact she had hoped he would build one someday from the ground up. I am sorry she did not get to see his dream become reality.

Roman's children also assumed I was going to try to take from him all the money he had gotten from the sale of his property. I remember being really hurt by that because his children didn't even bother to get to know me. Had they done so, they would have known better. I had even suggested Roman divide up the money and just give it to his children, since we didn't need it. Roman told me not to worry about the children. He said he was not giving them any money because he had big plans and if there was any left when he died they might, or might not, get what was left.

Roman and I spoke about marriage, but we agreed that neither of us wished to take that road. However, we did want a commitment from each other and we decided we would be engaged for life. That was enough to bind our relationship forever without the wedding. It was a mutual agreement. Marriage never worked for me. Maybe this time my relationship would be different. Roman did not want to marry again, either.

As the years whisked by, Roman started to talk about buying land to build our log house on. We looked at several properties, but nothing seemed to click. We decided since the land was already available, he would build on the south corner of the fifty-five acres that he already owned.

We looked at many plans and decided to take a plan and revise it to what we wanted. In the summer of 1998, Roman began the building process for our new log home. I continued to work and make the long drive every day.

Often on my long drive to work, I would pray. I was so thankful for all the good things that had come to me. I had a wonderful man in my life, a good job, a beautiful engagement ring, a nice car, and a wonderful big log house. I was at peace. Was there anything better than that? I was so grateful to finally be happy. If there was anything else that I could have, could I please find a way to help Roman build the new log house?

In September of 1998, Roman sold the house in Two Rivers and we moved into the apartment above David, in the family homestead. David said we could live there rent-free in exchange for farm duties. Roman liked the farm lifestyle so didn't mind moving cows and helping with repairs. Technically everything still belonged to Roman, as David had not paid for it all. He was merely hanging on, renting month-to-month.

When Roman had time, he started working on the new log house. In the fall Roman was to have eye surgery, so construction would have to stop until he got the clearance to return to carpentry. We figured it would be spring before he could work on it again. He put in long hours to get as much done as he could.

That month I was involved with the budget process at work. We were discussing who might be nearing retirement age. I asked my boss what the youngest age someone could retire was. He told me it was fifty-eight. I was that old, I thought, and why didn't I know that! I knew what I would do. I would go to the personnel department and talk to them about retiring. Wasn't this what I had prayed for?

Over the next few weeks I spoke to the people who would tell me where I would be financially if I retired. At first it was bad. I couldn't live on what they offered me. Then I spoke to them again and they offered me a better deal, but they said that this amount was all I could get. I would not get a dime more, even if I worked the next five years. *Wow! This was my way out. I could retire, have a monthly income, and yet be home to help Roman build our house. My body was at work, but my mind was already at home building with him.* I decided to go for it and stopped working at Kohler Company in December of 1998. I was officially retired in June of 1999, after twenty-one years with them. I will always be grateful to Kohler Company for giving me a chance as a co-op student.

My children had a surprise retirement party for me on January 30, 1999. I cried. I was so proud of my children and the good adults that they had all become. What more could a mother ask for? They even went so far as to write a letter to the president of the company asking him to attend. I read the letter and cried again. This is what it said:

Dear Sir:

Our mother, Geri Allen, has recently retired from your company after 20+ years of employment. We are hosting a retirement party in her honor on January 30, 1999.

We realize that you are extremely busy and your calendar is very full; however, we write hoping you would consider attending this event, even if it is only for a few minutes.

When she began working for your company, she was a single mother of seven children. She made many personal sacrifices for us over the years and we want very much to show her our appreciation and pride.

Due to the short notice, we understand if you are unable to attend and thank you for taking the time to read this letter.

Respectfully,

The Children of Geri Allen

I felt truly honored and blessed that my children felt this way about me after all they had gone through because of my relationships. My heart swelled with pride. The president of the company did not show up at the party, but that was all right. I was honored that they went so far as to invite him.

In the next few months, David and Roman would often argue about how to maintain the farm and how to care for the cows. Their arguments became a daily issue. Roman would tell me how David called him cruel names in front of his (David's) friends while he was trying to fix equipment. Several times David threatened to call the police and have us thrown off the property. I guess he forgot who actually owned the property. These were bad times for all of us.

During the year of 1999, Roman and I worked together feverishly on the log house. The sooner we could move in and get away from David the better. The years hadn't changed David any; he was still a bully. We got up every day and went to the job site. By the end of the year, December 20, 1999, to be exact, we moved into our new log house. We would be spending New Years Eve, the millennium new year, in our new creation. David wanted us out anyway because he wanted to rent the upstairs apartment. I felt sorry for whoever moved in and had that bully for a landlord.

That very first night in our new house I was happy and I was at peace. I take the time to thank God every day for blessing me with so much.

I truly wished things could have been better between Roman and his oldest son David, but it only got worse. David actually told Roman that he no longer had a father that he (Roman) should have died instead of his mother. *How cruel can a son be to his father!*

Time would pass and all of a sudden they would be talking to each other again. It was as if cruel words were never spoken, but I am certain they were never forgotten. Then as usual another argument would erupt, and again David would make threats. I could only console Roman and hope it would pass. I wonder sometimes if David realizes that he wouldn't have what he has today, if it were not for his dad's help. But as I said that story is another book.

Years have gone by and David is married now and has a son of his own. Now he knows what it is like to be a father. Roman and David are presently working on making a better father-son relationship.

24
Apology

On June 28, 2003, Todd Lisowe, Bob's oldest son and his bride, Jenny, had a wedding reception for family and friends. He and his bride had been married earlier on a tropical island and now wanted to share their day.

When we received the invitation, I was apprehensive about seeing all those people from my past again. I thought about it almost every day and anticipated what I would say to all of them.

When Roman and I arrived at the reception, I immediately saw Joan and her family and some of Bob's family at the very next table. They were all talking together. I thought to myself that this was a good sign, a sign of peace between the families.

After we ate, Roman and I talked with members of my family as I gazed at the crowd. I saw Joan get up and walk toward our direction. I was wondering if she would be able to come to speak to me freely, but she never looked in our direction. I was relatively certain she knew I was there, but unsure what I might do or say to her. Joan stopped five chairs down to speak to Terry's wife, Ann, and others who were sitting there. She was facing the other way with her back to us and the chair next to her was empty.

My heart was racing because I still had all those feelings inside me. I decided if I was going to talk to her, I needed to go now or I wouldn't do it. I took a deep breath and got off my chair. *OK, God, I'm up, now I need to make my feet move*, I prayed. I pulled the chair away from the table beside her, sat down, touched her shoulder, and said, "Joan." She turned to look at me and we just automatically gave each other a hug. I don't even remember who made the first gesture; it didn't matter.

I looked at her and said, "Joan, I am truly sorry. I am sorry for all the hurt and pain so many people suffered. I am sorry I ever brought Ken back to Wisconsin. Perhaps if I hadn't, it wouldn't have gone as far as it did. I am sorry you got caught up in the smooth-talking mind games." Joan replied that I had nothing to be sorry about and that she had had other problems at the time and had made some bad choices. Tears welled up in her eyes. She said she wished she could explain how she felt when her daughter-in-law, Ann, had called her and read the e-mail I had sent to her. The one where I had said I had forgiven her (Joan), and that I knew she was a good mother. She said she cried and cried. I told her again that I was truly sorry. Joan replied that I had misunderstood—they were tears of joy! Tears of relief that I had forgiven her! She said she still had the e-mail and looked at it every once in awhile. It made her feel better. She said she always wondered if I would ever be able to forgive her. I replied I had forgiven her many years ago and in fact I wanted to speak to her at Terry's wedding, but the timing wasn't right. The pain was still too fresh in all the families involved. I stated that I was very uncomfortable at Terry's wedding. I said there was her side of the family and Bob's side of the family and that my family and I were right in the middle. Joan agreed it would not have been the right time.

I told Joan that Ken was a manipulator and a con man and he knew how to work people's minds to go in the direction he wanted them to go. I told her I understood what she had been through, because I had lived it, too. I told her I knew she loved her boys and knew that she would have wanted to take them along. I also told her I knew that Ken would have said that they wouldn't get very far if she took her two sons and he took his two girls. Joan told me that was exactly what he had said. The never-ending mind games!

Joan told me Ken was a player. She worked, and he played. She said he had remarried just three short months after their divorce into a family that had lots of money. I told her it did not surprise me because that was what he was, a gold digger, a mind controller, and an abuser. But what goes around comes around, as they say, and one day he will get his. Sometime, somewhere he will get paid back for hurting so many people.

Joan said she had made so many mistakes and so many bad choices. I told her it was not her fault alone and to just let it go. The kids were all grown and good people and those that couldn't get beyond it have their own problems.

I asked Joan if she was happy now and she nodded. She said her husband treats her very well. She said that when she met him, she told him outright he may not want to be with her if he knew the whole story about everything. She told him the truth about everything, and he told her to just let it go and move on. He said that you can't change your past but that you can mold your future. He sounded like a special man.

Joan said if it wasn't for Terry's wife, Ann, she didn't know how she would have been able to go on over the years. She is such a special lady and so good for Terry. She was happy for both her sons.

Joan told me that Ken was such a liar and that he told so many lies that he convinced her they were true. She said that because of him she had even told lies to her own family, which she had never done before. There was the mind control thing again. Boy, he was good at it. He was such a user of people. I was very confident some day he would get his due.

Joan told me she looked at the obituaries in the newspaper every day to see if his name was listed. I told her I was surprised someone hadn't shot him by now and if she did see his name listed in the obituary to please call me. I told her we could get together and raise a glass in a salute. We both laughed.

I told Joan I would not keep her any longer, but that there was still so much to say. So much to talk about! But it would have to be another time. Joan commented Terry's wife was going to try to help her learn the computer and when she figured out how to send e-mail she would send one to me. I said that would be nice. We hugged again, and she got up and left.

I took a deep breath and said silently, *Thank you, Lord, for giving me the courage and the words to speak to her. It was something I had wanted to do for such a very long time. Thank you for giving me the place to end this. Instead of blaming her, I told her I was sorry for causing so much pain.*

I went to speak to Cindy, my daughter, and Ann was there by her. She looked at me and said I was so cute. She said she thought Joan went pale and was going to faint when she turned around and saw me. I said I hadn't noticed anyone was watching.

Laura told me later she was sitting very close when I approached Joan. She said she had to get up and leave when she heard Joan talking about her dad. That comment caught me off guard. She said she had formed her own opinion of what her dad was like and did not want to hear any more. It was sad she never had a good relationship with her dad but I am sure she was better off not knowing him.

I had been certain Laura had no emotion about the whole thing because she was so young. But when she told me she had to get up and leave when Joan was talking about her dad, I was not so sure anymore that she wasn't affected, too.

Laura, now thirty-four, married a great guy whose name was Brian Nitka. They have two boys, Alexander and Justin. She works for a national chain of craft supply stores as a managerial assistant. If anyone in our family has the normal family life, it is she. Laura has supported my decision to publish this book.

Diana asked if Joan and I were going to be coffee drinking buddies now. I understood her hostility but thought it was a rude comment that didn't deserve a response. Diana hadn't been able to get past her childhood pain and may never be able to get over it. I am certain she will never forgive Ken for anything. Her hate for him has burned very strong and even in her adult years she fans the flame. Her pain is still very deep.

Diana, now forty-four, is presently unmarried, although she and Eric are still very close and seem to want to be with each other. Maybe some day they can reunite. I am very proud to say she is a sheriff's department deputy. She has two children, Amanda and Michael. In many crucial ways, her life has not paralleled mine and I am grateful for that. I truly hope that someday she writes about her life as well. She did not want me to write this book. I guess it is because she is embarrassed that we lived like we did, and I am sure she remembers much more than I wrote about.

Cindy has let the pain go and considers the past the past. She sees no need to dwell on it. She doesn't remember her dad and has brushed him away just like he did her. She said those things happened to us, not because of us, and we should not be ashamed of being survivors.

Cindy, now thirty-seven, is married to her soul mate Jeff Lenz. She has five children, Chelsie, Dustan, Brittney, Deliah, and Alan Jeffery, or A. J. as they call him. Last year she became a grandmother. Chelsie had a baby girl named Payten. I am a great-grandmother now. Cindy seems to be happy with her life and her family. She works for a large national insurance company and has her own Internet business, Little Devils LLC. She read a copy of my draft manuscript and has encouraged me all the way to get this book published.

Leary has moved on and none of it fazes him any more. He has the attitude that it is all in the past, let it stay there! He read the rough draft of this book and stated he remembered a lot of abuse that I didn't write about. I can only say I wrote about what I remembered. He is, however, encouraging me to get this book published.

Leary, now forty-two, is married to a lovely lady named Brenda, and they have three children: Crystal, Tequila, and Cameron. Leary is working with the National Guard and may get shipped out to Iraq in the next few months. I will surely be praying for his safe return.

Michael was not at the wedding reception because he couldn't get away from work and school. However, Michael is very bitter when it comes to Ken and swears he will get revenge someday for the abuse he suffered. He hopes to have an opportunity to beat him to a pulp. I don't know what his reaction would have been to Joan had he seen her.

Michael, now thirty-nine, is unmarried with no children. He lives in California and likes the single life. I sometimes wonder if he chose the single life because he saw what married life was like for me and how hard it was to raise children. He should have been a model, too, with his slim build and blond hair. He likes surfing and has a golden tan. He worked for a major airline company for many years and traveled all over the world. He is presently going to college and working as an electrician's apprentice. He seems happy.

Michael feels I didn't get the whole truth of the abuse out there in the book. I can only write what I remembered. Perhaps I suppressed memories of both mental and physical abuse. I am not leaving anything out on purpose.

I was told Terry Lisowe has suppressed his childhood memories and doesn't remember much of it. I also understand he doesn't like to talk about it. I hope that doesn't harm him someday. Although he had a copy of the rough draft of this book I do not believe he read it.

Terry, now thirty-seven, is married to a beautiful lady named Ann, and they have two boys, David and Brock. Terry is an electrician and works for a local electrical company. He is a good man with truly good family values, like his dad.

It appears Todd Lisowe, Bob's older son, has forgiven his mother and is at peace with it all. He has grown to be a good family man as well. He said he appreciated the fact that I mentioned the family gatherings at his grandparent's house when he was growing up. Those were always special days for him.

Todd, now thirty-nine, is married to a beautiful lady named Jenny, and has a daughter Amaya Kate. He works for a local bank. Todd had a rough draft of this book to read, and when he finished it, he called me. He said, he had thought he couldn't respect me anymore than he already did, but after reading the manuscript he found he could. I am honored that he is encouraging me to get this book published.

Both Todd and Terry seem happy with their lives and their families. I can only pray they will always be happy and that their dad Bob is their guardian angel, watching over them.

I am very proud of all my children and the fact that they turned into good, responsible adults. They seem to have gotten through it all with their heads held high. I pray they will all have peace and happiness in their futures. They all have high family values and are very close to each other. I know they will truly care for and be there for each other during any crisis. I guess I wasn't such a bad mother after all.

I have told all my children to shake Ken's hand if they ever see him and to thank him for leaving. We were all better for it. He is expecting a punch in the nose because he has also not forgotten what he did. But a grateful handshake will take him to his knees. It will reduce him to the small, unimportant, insignificant person he really is.

For me it is a final chapter in a world of pain and anger. I can close this book with peace in my heart knowing God gave me the courage to forgive. He led me through these experiences so I could write what I have written. It was his hand that helped me get it done.

As we were leaving the reception, it was really good to see Bob's and Joan's families talking with each other. I hope that the peace between the two families was a sign of forgiveness.

I can sleep tonight knowing that even if Joan can't forgive herself, I have. I can't begin to describe how good that feels. I am finally at peace with it all.

I have survived the pain and sorrow. I have been through the mill of love, and I am a better person for it. Turmoil and heartache can prove to be valuable lessons and assets. It is hard to understand when it is happening, and it is hard to understand why the pain has to be so severe to learn a lesson.

It seems there is a grand design for each of us, for our development. I went through all these particular trials for a reason. Now I can show someone else the value of strife and struggles. It is my purpose on this earth. If I can help just one person then I have accomplished the task God gave to me in my life. There is hope for everyone and a better place ahead.

Life does not come with guarantees for happiness or against heartaches and pain. Be happy and love your family and God. Be true to yourself. Everything else you can overcome.

I am sixty-five now and finally living my life, as I always wanted it to be. I am moving on with my life with Roman. He is a good man and, with God's help, we will live the rest of our lives together on this earth in peace and happiness as we do now. We moved away from Wisconsin because of the cold weather and high taxes and now live in lower Missouri. We have been together for eleven and a half years. Even though I am not living in Wisconsin, I will always love and be connected to my children.

My mom, Emma, is now eighty-seven. She is a great-great-grandmother and is living with us in Missouri. We love having her here, and she has a better quality of life being away from Wisconsin and the damp, cold weather. I am proud to be able to help her and hope she has many more years with us. She has supported my writing this book from the day she read the rough draft of it. Her will and her strength are what kept me going.

978-0-595-38691-8
0-595-38691-1

Printed in the United States
57994LVS00006B/16